CHAUCER AND THE LITURGY

by

Beverly Boyd

DORRANCE & COMPANY

Philadelphia

To

Francis X. FitzGibbon

"A bettre preest I trowe that nowher noon ys."

General Prologue, 524

PREFACE

The discussions which follow explore topics concerning Chaucer's references to the liturgy, both for their meaning and for their light on the poet's thinking. Quotations from his works, necessarily very numerous, are from F. N. Robinson's Second Edition (Boston, 1957), and lines from the *Canterbury Tales* are here numbered according to the order of the tales followed in this edition. It has seemed desirable to present quotations from other Middle English literature according to similar editorial methods. Symbols for *and* have therefore been expanded. The symbols þ (thorn) and ȝ (yogh) have been removed in favor of, respectively, *th* and either *y* or *gh*. The scribal *i, j,* and *u, v* have been normalized. Modern English capitalization has been introduced. Where possible, I have used editions in which such changes are already made. Otherwise, I have made them myself.

In dealing with Latin, differences between medieval spellings and the classical spellings preferred by some editors of liturgical books create problems which admit of no ready solution in the expansion of passages for which the sources provide only cues. The best compromise has seemed to be the use of translations along with the Latin cues. In presenting these cues and other Latin passages, scribal peculiarities have argued against the expansion of abbreviations beyond what has already been done in the editions here used. But *u, v* have been normalized, and capitalization has been introduced for proper nouns, proper adjectives, and words that begin sentences. Modern punctuation has been introduced, and abbreviations in titles have been silently expanded. These procedures will not satisfy everyone, but they will bring the materials within the reach of many who may wish to know how Chaucer felt about one of the most interesting aspects of life in the Middle Ages.

This study was begun in 1961, under a grant from the American Philosophical Society (Penrose Fund, Grant No. 2850) which enabled me to examine manuscripts in New York, London, and Oxford. I should like to express my thanks to the librarians of the Pierpont Morgan Library, the British Museum, Westminster Abbey, St. Paul's Cathedral (London), and the Bodleian Library, for the privilege of reading in their collections. In particular, I am indebted to A. R. B. Fuller, of St. Paul's Cathedral Library, for answering numerous questions pertaining to the calendar in MS. 1 and for obtaining for me the advice of Francis Wormald regarding the scribal handwriting. Acknowledgment is made to the Dean and Chapter of the Cathedral for permission to publish the calendar.

I should also like to express my thanks to S. J. P. van Dijk, O.F.M., for correspondence regarding the liturgy according to the Use of St. Paul's, to N. Wyman Storer, of the University of Kansas, for advice regarding medieval astronomy, and to John C. Broderick, of the Library of Congress, for help in locating material published abroad. Finally, I am grateful to the University of Kansas for a research grant in 1965–66, which has enabled me to bring this volume to completion.

Lawrence, Kansas   September, 1966

CONTENTS

I. THE SOURCES

Chaucer reports in his writings the customs of a society deeply influenced by the liturgy of the Roman Rite. The liturgy is in his pages because it was part of the way of life. For the poet's readers of another age, this aspect of his poetry and prose is involved in the history of religious controversy by the figure of John Wyclif. But Chaucer's references and allusions to the liturgy and his paraphrases of it also reveal things about him which have little connection with the reformer and Chaucer's possible sympathy with his cause. An exploration of Chaucer's literary treatment of the liturgy is necessary not only for factual information about the passages in his works where such references occur but for light on his personal attitudes toward an important aspect of the medieval scene.

Prerequisite to such a study is documentary evidence of the liturgy as Chaucer had it in mind when he wrote about it. This may seem too obvious to require assertion. Yet criteria for identifying the necessary evidence are conspicuously lacking. Notes and articles on particular problems have employed a great many sources, including the personal experience of those who today practice Catholicism under the Roman Rite. Certainly, this kind of knowledge is valuable background to bring to the study of medieval literature. But the liturgy has been through centuries of revision and standardization since the Middle Ages, and it was not in those times the seamless garment often supposed. Not every liturgical source pertaining to the Roman Rite will provide the kind of evidence needed for a correct reading of Chaucer's allusions to the Church's ceremonies, even if English and medieval.

Medieval liturgical books are extant in considerable numbers. The problems such books present to the reader wishing to use

1

them in connection with literature are complex. For one thing, they exhibit among themselves variation which can be extensive. For another, they assume familiarity with the Church's services in the most literal sense, so that often they consist mostly of cues and rubrics (directions). While dealing with them cannot be made simple, it is certainly possible to establish criteria for deciding which are valid in connection with Chaucer. After that, the rubrics are usually enough to explain differences from more recent service books according to the Roman Rite. These, however, must be approached with caution as far as specific comparisons are concerned, for the liturgy has been greatly revised in the mid-twentieth century and the changes are too recent to be regarded as common knowledge.

Before considering the problem of sources, the term "liturgy" requires explanation. As applied to the Roman Rite, it means the official public worship of the Church in contrast with private prayer. In western Europe during the Middle Ages, the liturgy consisted of the mass or eucharistic service, the services of the canonical hours, those for the administration of other sacraments besides the eucharist, and various additional rituals of consecration and blessing. But there was more than one traditional set of services, each set known as a rite. Rites were usually associated with particular geographical areas. Even today, there are several under the jurisdiction of the papacy at Rome, though its own liturgy, the Roman Rite, is the one most prevalent.

The quest for information about these matters in connection with Chaucer necessarily follows historical lines, beginning with the fact that the early popes did not enforce their own rite as bishops of Rome upon all persons and organizations under their authority. Most of western Europe originally (or at least as long ago as the earliest records) followed the Gallican Rite, about which very little historical information is known. Though some have supposed that it came into Gaul from Antioch, its origin is actually obscure, and it seems to have been a type of liturgy rather than a single set of services.[1] If there was any papal aspiration toward liturgical unity by the time of Gregory the Great

2

(ca. 540–604), it is not revealed in his transactions with St. Augustine, for Bede says in his *Ecclesiastical History* that he (Gregory) instructed the missionary bishop to take for the Church in Britain what seemed to him suitable, whether from Rome or from Gaul.[2] While some movement toward unity is implied by the controversy over the date of Easter settled at Whitby in 664, the original impetus toward adoption of Roman ceremonial customs is ascribed to the Frankish kings, who sent to Rome for texts of the liturgy in use there and imposed them upon their realm. The books involved were sacramentaries, which contained only the celebrant's parts of the mass and other services.[3]

Since there was little central control over these matters, there was likewise little to prevent the addition of local ceremonial customs, old and new, to what was specified in the sacramentaries. Thus, although by the twelfth century the Roman Rite had replaced other liturgies almost everywhere in the West, it was subject to variation in minor aspects of ceremonial at both the diocesan and monastic levels, and liturgical books, having to accommodate them, were not uniform. All such variants within the Roman Rite are known as derived rites or uses. In its broadest sense, the term "use" came to include the whole corpus of regulations pertaining to the liturgy and its personnel as affecting a cathedral and its chapter of canons (staff of clergy) and consequently its diocese. The term also applied in the same sense to the ceremonial customs of religious orders and their churches. While most uses were eventually abolished, this was not until after the Reformation. Their existence complicates literary allusions to the Church's services, and the matter has not received sufficient attention in that regard.

Like other places, England had its own derived rites. The most important one in Chaucer's time was the Use of Salisbury, better known as the Use of Sarum (the abbreviated form of the Latin *Sarisburium*). Tradition ascribes its composition to St. Osmund, a Norman nobleman whom William the Conqueror appointed bishop of Salisbury (1078).[4] The fact that it was more elaborate in carrying out the services of the Roman Rite than were other

3

English uses can be readily seen from William Maskell's parallel-text edition of the mass according to the uses of Sarum, Bangor, Hereford, York, and Rome.[5] Its ritual must have appealed to something in the times, for it rapidly became the dominant liturgical influence, not only in England but throughout the British Isles. Most opposition to it was in the north of England. By Chaucer's time, much of the southern half of the country had either borrowed from it extensively or adopted it outright.[6]

In the process of changing to a different use, or even of revising a use under Salisbury influence, old liturgical books became obsolete unless they were corrected, sometimes extensively. Many were doubtless scrapped. All this must have been troublesome and expensive. The clergy, too, were put to the inconvenience of learning new ways of carrying out their ceremonial duties. These problems came into focus at about the middle of the fourteenth century, when the Sarum Use was itself revised.[7] Its ordinal, a book of cues and rubrics that served as a guide to its service books, drew complaints from Wyclif. He protests in the tract "Of Feigned Contemplative Life,"

> Also the ordynalle of Salisbury lettith moche prechynge of the gospel; for folis chargen that more than the maundementis of God and to studie and teche Cristis gospel; for yif a man faile in his ordynale men holden that grete synne and reproven hym therof faste, but yif a preste breke the hestis of God men chargen that litel or nought; and so yif prestis seyn here matynes, masse and evensong aftir Salisbury usse, thei hem self and othere men demen it is ynowgh, though thei neither preche ne teche the hestis of God and the gospel.

He continues,

> Hou doren synful folis chargen Cristis prestis with so moche novelrie, and evermore cloute more to, that thei may not frely do Goddis ordynaunce? For the Jewis in the olde lawe haden not so manye seremonyes of sacri-

4

fices ordeyned bi God as prestis han now righttis and reulis maade of synful men.

He concludes,

A lord, yif alle the studie and traveile that men han now abowte Salisbury uss with multitude of newe costy portos, antifeners, graielis, and alle othere bokis weren turned in-to makynge of Biblis. . . .[8]

It should be noted that Wyclif was from Yorkshire, where there was in any case strong resistance to Salisbury liturgical customs.

Although Chaucer's career took him traveling and prevented permanent association with the parochial aspects of any single place, his life is closely connected with London, the Diocese of St. Paul's, and it is to this diocese that one should expect to look for the liturgy as he knew it best. Officially, London had its own derived rite until 1414, some years after Chaucer's death (1400). William Dugdale summarizes a document which gives notice of the change to Sarum Use:

And *in Anno* MCCCCXIV. (2.H.5) Oct. xv. *Richard Clifford,* then Bishop of **London,** by the consent of the Dean and Chapter, ordained, that from the first day of *December* following, beginning then at *Vespers,* the solemn Celebration of divine service therein, which before that time had been according to a peculiar forme antiently used, and called *Usus Sancti Pauli,* should thenceforth be conformable to that of the Church of **Salisbury,** for all Canonicall hours, both night and day.[9]

There is strong indication that the Use of St. Paul's had been losing its hold upon the Diocese for some time. The most sensitive aspect of any use was its patron saints, and in 1386, Bishop Robert Braybrooke found it necessary to order his archdeacon to see that the patronal feasts, then falling into neglect, were properly observed: the Conversion of St. Paul (25 January), the

Commemoration of St. Paul (30 June: the day after the feast he shares with St. Peter), the Deposition of St. Erkenwald (30 April: the day commemorating the removal of his relics to a shrine above the high altar in St. Paul's), and the Translation of St. Erkenwald (14 November: his anniversary, transferred from another date to avoid conflict with an important feast).[10] St. Erkenwald, an early bishop of London who died ca. 690, is familiar as the subject of a Middle English alliterative poem which may have been composed under circumstances related to Bishop Braybrooke's concern about the saint's feasts.[11] To what extent Sarum Use had replaced local customs in the Diocese before 1414 is not known. But in a place like London where there were many transients, many benefices outside the bishop's immediate jurisdiction, and many cross-currents of thought, it would have been impossible to prevent the influence of a vigorous liturgical movement. There can be no doubt that the Use of Sarum should figure largely in any attempt to deal with Chaucer's liturgical allusions.

Under ordinary circumstances, a study of this area would be approached through a comparison of Sarum Use and the Use of St. Paul's. This, however, is no longer possible, for the Use of St. Paul's is one of many medieval derived rites known today only because other documents mention them. Its disappearance is probably the result of scribal correction and rubrication, certainly after Clifford's proclamation of 1414, and perhaps even earlier. The few scraps of the old use which remain reveal nothing that could be of assistance in reconstructing ceremonial customs.[12] Thus, the Use of St. Paul's must be written off as lost. Books of worship according to the Use of Sarum are the best available evidence of the Roman Rite as it was in Medieval England to serve as a basis for investigating Chaucer's references to the liturgy.

NOTES TO CHAPTER I

[1] Adrian Fortescue, "Liturgy," *The Catholic Encypclopedia* (New York, 1910), IX, 311(col. 1). See also Henry Jenner,

"Gallican Rite," *CE*, VI, 357(col. 1)–365(col. 2). The Gallican Mass is described by L. Duchesne, *Christian Worship*, trans. M. L. McClure, 5th ed. (London, 1949), pp. 189–227. Duchesne's study discusses the history of the liturgy up to the time of Charlemagne.

[2] *Venerabilis Baedae historia ecclesiastica gentis Anglorum*, in *Venerabilis Baedae opera historica*, ed. Charles Plummer (Oxford, 1896), I, 49.

[3] For discussion concerning sacramentaries, see Fortescue, "Liturgical Books," *CE*, IX, 297(col. 2)–300(col. 1).

[4] The tradition is discussed by Daniel Rock, *The Church of Our Fathers*, 2nd ed., IV (London, 1904), 135–38; and by W. H. Frere, *The Use of Sarum*, I (Cambridge, 1898), xv–xx; for critical comment on Rock's work, see Frere, liii–lvi.

[5] *The Ancient Liturgy of the Church of England*, 3rd ed. (Oxford, 1882). The best edition of the Sarum Missal is that of J. Wickham Legg (Oxford, 1916).

[6] A historical outline is given by Frere, xxi–xxxvii; II (1901), xxvii–xxxii.

[7] Frere, II, xxii ff.

[8] Ed. F. D. Matthew, *The English Works of Wyclif*, Early English Text Soc., O. S., No. 74 (London, 1880), pp. 192–94.

[9] *The History of St. Paul's Cathedral in London* (London, 1658), p. 22.

[10] W. Sparrow Simpson, *Documents Illustrating the History of S. Paul's Cathedral* (Westminster, 1880), pp. xx–xxi.

[11] "St. Erkenwald," ed. Henry L. Savage, *Yale Studies in English*, LXXII (New Haven, 1926).

[12] (1) MS. 1, St. Paul's Cathedral, London: a psalter with a calendar (see below, pp. 22–3, and Plates 1–12); (2) Additional

7

MS. 5,810, British Museum: an eighteenth century transcript of a lost original containing collects for the feasts of St. Paul and St. Erkenwald, ed. Simpson, pp. xxi–xxix; 17–40; (3) the Ordinal of Barking Abbey (University College, Oxford, MS. 169, copied ca. 1394–1404: Bodleian Library), ed. J. B. L. Tolhurst, *The Ordinale and Customary of the Benedictine Nuns of Barking Abbey*, Henry Bradshaw Soc., Nos. 65, 66 (London, 1926, 1927); an appended document (fol. 219) states that mass is to be according to the Use of St. Paul's, but the information is of no value without a missal according to that use.

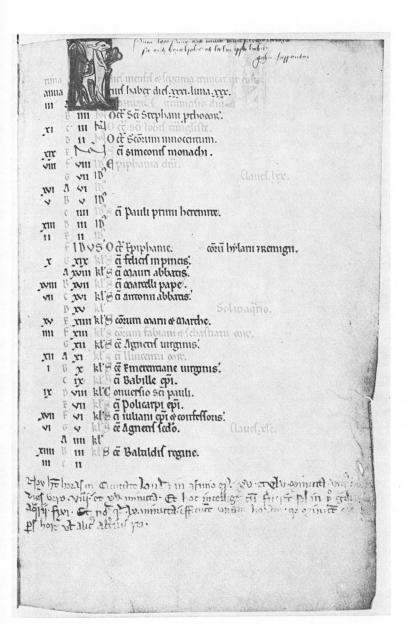

PLATE 1

The Calendar of St. Paul's Cathedral MS. 1: January

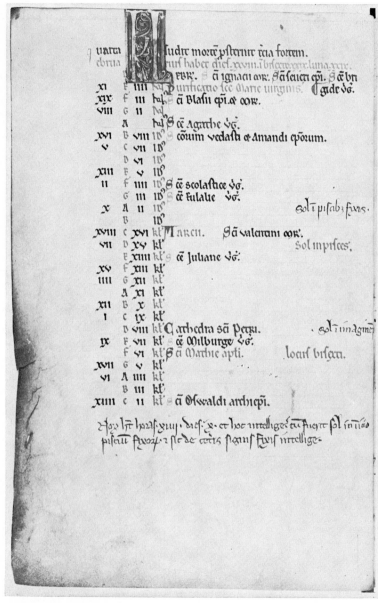

PLATE 2

The Calendar of St. Paul's Cathedral MS. 1: February

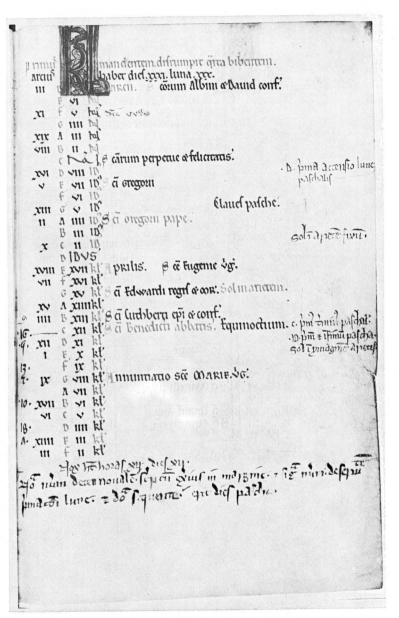

PLATE 3

The Calendar of St. Paul's Cathedral MS. 1: March

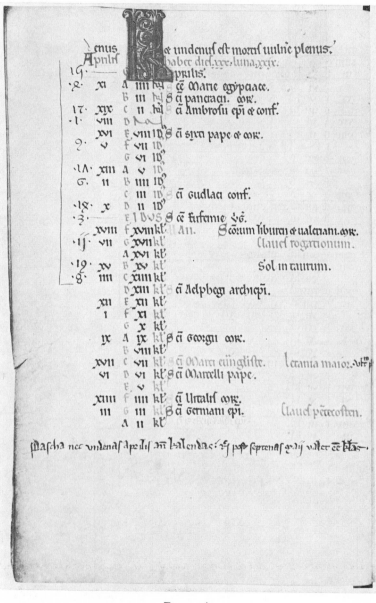

PLATE 4

The Calendar of St. Paul's Cathedral MS. 1: April

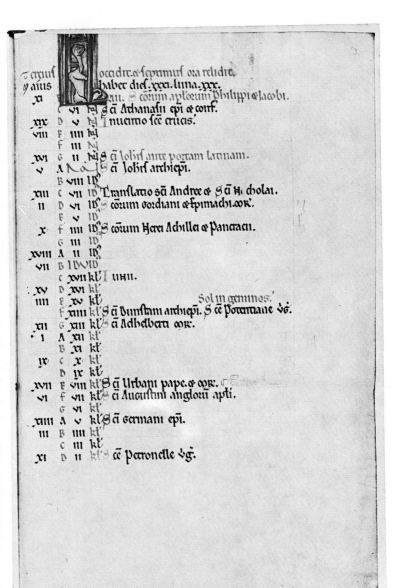

occidit: & septimus ora relidit.
habet dies .xxxi. luna .xxx.
Kl. mai. ⚜ coium aploeum Philippi & Iacobi.
.xix. | c | vi | Kl | S̄ ā Athanasii epī & cōnf.
.viii. | D | v | Kl | Inuentio scē crucis.
| E | iiii | Kl |
| F | iii | Kl |
.xvi. | G | ii | Kl | S̄ ā Iohīs ante portam latinam.
.v. | A | | Kl | S̄ ā Iohīs archiepī.
| B | viii | Id |
.xiii. | c | vii | Id | Translatio sā Andree & S̄ ā Nicholai.
.ii. | D | vi | Id | cōium Gordiani & Epimachi mr̄.
| E | v | Id |
.x. | F | iiii | Id | S̄ cōium Nerei Achillei & Pancratii.
| G | iii | Id |
.xviii. | A | ii | Id |
.vii. | B | Id |
| c | xvii | Kl | mai.
.xv. | D | xvi | Kl |
.iiii. | E | xv | Kl | Sol in geminos.
| F | xiiii | Kl | S̄ ā Dunstani archiepī. S̄ cē Potentiane vḡ.
.xii. | G | xiii | Kl | S̄ ā Adhelberti mr̄.
.i. | A | xii | Kl |
| B | xi | Kl |
.ix. | c | x | Kl |
| D | ix | Kl |
.xvii. | E | viii | Kl | S̄ ā Urbani pape & mr̄.
.vi. | F | vii | Kl | S̄ ā Augustini anglorū aplī.
| G | vi | Kl |
.xiiii. | A | v | Kl | S̄ ā Germani epī.
.iii. | B | iiii | Kl |
| c | iii | Kl |
.xi. | D | ii | Kl | cē Petronelle vḡ.

PLATE 5

The Calendar of St. Paul's Cathedral MS. 1: May

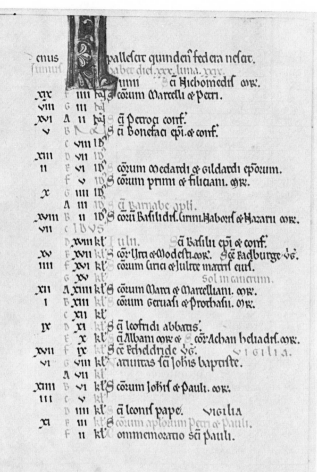

enus   pallescat quinden̄ fedeta nesat.

sumus   haber diel.xxx. luna. xxx.

          iiui   ā Nichomedis conf̄.

xix   f   iiii ka̅ſ co̅rum Marcelli & petri.

viii   G   iii ka̅ſ

xvi   A   ii ka̅ſ ā petroc̄ conf.

   v   B   kal̄ S ā boneſaci epi. & conf.

        c   viii Id̄

xiii   D   vii Id̄

  ii   E   vi Id̄   co̅rum medardi & gildardi epo̅rum.

       f   v   Id̄ S co̅rum primi & filiciani. ∞ℜ.

   x   G   iiii Id̄

       A   iii Id̄ ā barnabe apli.

xviii B   ii   Id̄ S co̅ru Basilidıſ.Cirini.Nabo̅rıſ &Nazarıi co̅ℜ.

vii   c   Id̄vs

       D   xviii ka̅ſ Iuln.   S ā basilii epi & conf.

xv   E   xvii ka̅ſ S co̅r Uici & modeſti.co̅ℜ.   Sc̄e ſadburge v̄g.

iiii   f   xvi ka̅ſ co̅rum Cirici & Julitte mart̄rıſ eiuſ.

       G   xv   ka̅ſ   Sol in cancrum.

xii   A   xiiii ka̅ſ S co̅rum Marci & Marcelliani. co̅ℜ.

  i   B   xiii ka̅ſ co̅rum Geruaſi & prochaſii. ∞ℜ.

       c   xii   ka̅ſ

ix   D   xi   ka̅ſ S ā leoſridi abbatıſ.

       E   x   ka̅ſ ā Albani co̅ℜ &   co̅r Achan heliadrſ.co̅ℜ.

xvii f   ix   ka̅ſ Sc̄e Etheldride v̄g.   vigilia.

vi   G   viii ka̅ſ natiuitas ſc̄i Johıs baptıſte.

       A   vii ka̅ſ

xiii   B   vi   ka̅ſ S co̅rum Johıſ & pauli. co̅ℜ.

iii   c   v   ka̅ſ

       D   iiii ka̅ſ ā leonıſ pape.   vigilia

xi   E   iii   ka̅ſ S co̅rum aplo̅rum petri & pauli.

       f   ii   ka̅ſ ommemoracio ſc̄i pauli.

PLATE 6

The Calendar of St. Paul's Cathedral MS. 1: June

Jrcleq | mnſ maccſe uiln. deanſ labefactat.
ſuluſ | haber dieſ. xxei. luna. xxx.
xix | ulu. O cē ſa lobiſ bapriſte.
v111 | A vi hɔ ſ cōũ proceſſi ⁊ ꝙartiniani. ꝙ̃ ſ ā ſwenduni.
| B v hɔ
xvi | c 111 hɔ Tranſlano ſcī ꝙartini epi ⁊ conſ.
v | D 111 hɔ
| E 11 hɔ Ocē Apſouum ꝑetn ⁊ pauli.
xiii | F Nɔ Tranſlacio ſa cho me ꝙ̃
11 | G v111 iⁱ
| A v11 iⁱ
x | B v1 iⁱ cōuim ſepten ſrꝛcuni.
| c v iⁱ
xviii | D 1111 iⁱ
v11 | E 111 iⁱ
| F 11 iⁱ
xv | G iⁱ v iⁱ
1111 | A xv11 kⱡ Auɡ. ſ ā ꝛuſtachii ſocaouunq; eiuſ.
| B xvi kⱡ ā kenelmi coꝛ.
x11 | c xv kⱡ ſol in leonem.
1 | D x1111 kⱡ
| F x111 kⱡ ſ cē ꝙargareꞇe ꝫc.
ix | F x11 kⱡ cē pꝛaxediſ uirg ⁊ coꝛ.
| G x1 kⱡ ſ cē ꝙarie magdalene.
xvii | A x kⱡ ā Apollinaꞇi coꝛ.
v1 | B ix kⱡ ſ cē xpine uɡ. vigilia.
| c v111 kⱡ ā Iacobi apⱡi. ā xpoſoꝛi coꝛ.
x1111 | D v11 kⱡ
111 | E v1 kⱡ cōuim ſepten doꝛnſeꞇniū. ⁊ beꞃꞇnciaſ.
| F v kⱡ ſ ā pantaleoniſ coꝛ. ſ ā ſanſoniſ epi.
x1 | G 1111 kⱡ cē ꝙarrhe ꝫc. cōuim feliaſ ſimpliaꝫ. fauſtini
xix | A 111 kⱡ ſ cōuim Abdon ⁊ ſennen. coꝛ.
| B 11 kⱡ ā ocꝛmaniſ epi ⁊ conſ.

PLATE 7

The Calendar of St. Paul's Cathedral MS. 1: July

Prima		negat fortem perdit sexta cohortem.
Augus		que habet dies .xxxi. luna .xxx.
vin	g	d uincula sci petri.
xvi	b iiii	g ci stephani pape & mr.
v	c iii	Inuentio corpis sci stephani.
	f ii	
xiii	g Non	s ci oswaldi regis & mr.
ii	A viii id	cöm sixti felicissimi & agapiti mr.
	B vii id	s ci Donati epi & mr.
x	c vi id	s ci Ciriaci martiris.
	D v id	s ci Romani mr. vigilia.
xviii	E iiii id	ci laurenti mr.
vii	F iii id	s ci tiburtii mr.
	G ii id	
xv	A IDVS	ci ypoliti mr.
iiii	b xix kl	Epi & mr. s ci Eusebii conf. vigilia.
	c xviii kl	Assumptio sce Marie uirginis.
xii	D xvii kl	
i	F xvi kl	Octaue sci laurenti.
	F xv kl	ci agapiti mr. Solin geminos.
ix	G xiiii kl	
	A xiii kl	
xvii	b xii kl	
vi	c xi kl	Oct sce Marie. & cor timothei & simphoriani mr
	D x kl	vigilia.
xiiii	E ix kl	s ci Bartholomei apli. & ci Audoeni epi.
iii	F viii kl	
	G vii kl	
xi	A vi kl	
	b v kl	ci Augustini epi & conf.
xix	c iiii kl	Decollatio sci Iohis baptiste. & ce sabine.sc
viii	D iii kl	cörum felicis & adaucti mr.
	E ii kl	

PLATE 8

The Calendar of St. Paul's Cathedral MS. 1: August

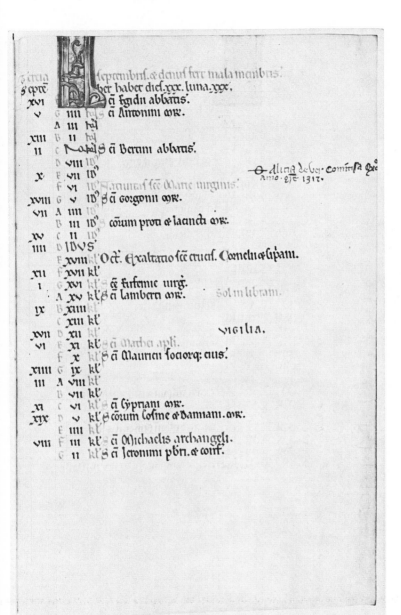

PLATE 9

The Calendar of St. Paul's Cathedral MS. 1: September

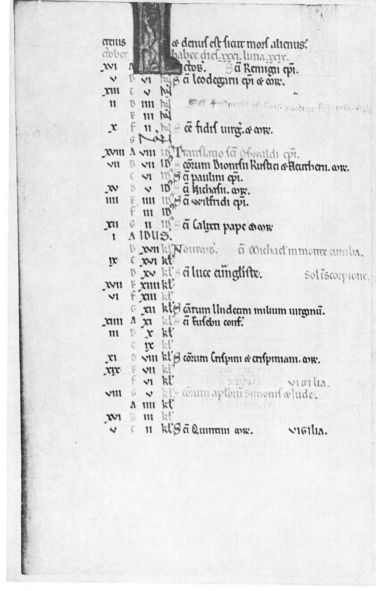

octuis &c denuſ eſt ſicut morſ alienuſ.
ctober habet dieſ.xxxi. luna.xxix.

xvi A ctoB. S̄ a̅ Remigii epi.
v B vi B a̅ leodegarii epi & cōr.
xiii C v
ii D iiii S̄ 4 quaſi of ſſonſ & uirtutib
E iii
x F ii, c̄e fidiſ uirg̅.& cōr.
G
xviii A viii id Tranſlatio ſc̄a Oſſualdi epi.
vii B vii id cōrum Dionſii Ruſtici & Eleuthern. cōr.
C vi id S̄ a̅ paulini epi.
xv D v id a̅ Michaſii. cōr.
iiii E iiii id a̅ ſ̄wilfridi epi.
F iii id
xii G ii id a̅ Calixti pape & cōr
i A IDUS.
B xvii kł Oureoſ. a̅ Michaeł in monte tumba.
ix C xvi kł
D xv kł a̅ luce euangliſte. Sol in ſcorpione.
xvii E xiiii kł
vi F xiii kł
G xii kł S̄ a̅rum Undecim milium uirginū.
xiiii A xi kł a̅ Euſebii conf.
iii B x kł
C ix kł
xi D viii kł S̄ cōrum Criſpini & criſpiniani. cōr.
xix E vii kł
F vi kł vigilia.
viii G v kł cōrum aploⁿ Simoniſ & Iude.
A iiii kł
xvi B iii kł
v C ii kł S̄ a̅ Quintini cōr. vigilia.

PLATE 10

The Calendar of St. Paul's Cathedral MS. 1: October

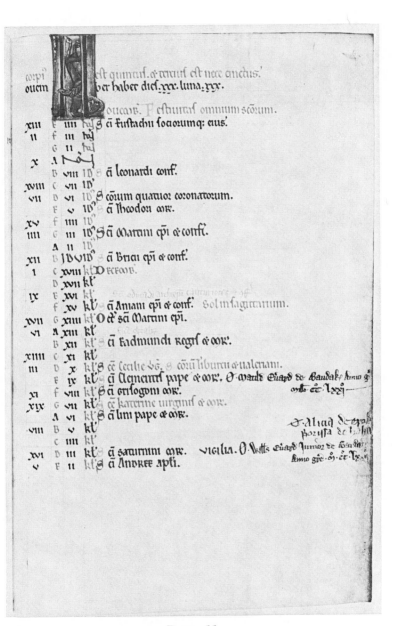

PLATE 11

The Calendar of St. Paul's Cathedral MS. 1: November

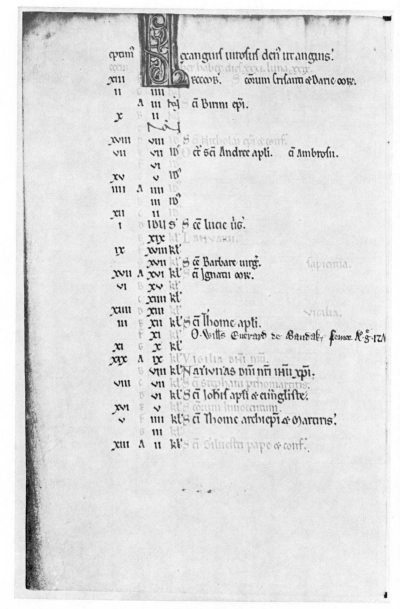

PLATE 12

The Calendar of St. Paul's Cathedral MS. 1: December

II. CHAUCER AND THE ECCLESIASTICAL CALENDAR

Chaucer writes of the Virgin Mary in the poem called "An ABC" (73–4), translated from Guillaume de Deguilleville's *Le Pèlerinage de Vie Humaine,*

> Kalenderes enlumyned ben thei
> That in this world ben lighted with thi name. . . .[1]

The reference is to ecclesiastically annotated calendars. Discussion of these comes early in the present study because the calendar is the principle by which the liturgy, its books, and its way of life were organized in the Middle Ages. Long before Chaucer's time, this had led to stylized liturgical annotation of the Julian calendar inherited from the Romans. Since most books of worship required calendars, these became the principal means of their preservation into modern times. Despite the fact that it is now customary to call them ecclesiastical calendars, the name is inexact. While there were almanacs and other scientific and pseudoscientific works in Chaucer's day which presented information about the date in various formats, the documents now called ecclesiastical calendars are not peculiar to books of worship, and they are so numerous, so heavily annotated with non-religious information, and at the same time so intrinsically representative of a way of life oriented to religious observances, that there can be no reasonable doubt that they represent the common medieval idea of a calendar.

Ecclesiastical calendars are best known today for their artwork and their rosters of saints, which are highly individualistic because the saints' days were largely a matter of local and monastic tradition. A great deal can be learned about the provenience of these calendars by examining their lists of saints.[2] Unfortunately, the studies that have been made from this point of view contain little basic introductory information, and the workings of the calendars are not self-explanatory.[3] While scholars concerned with Chaucer have combed them for the identities of the saints he mentions, the documents themselves have not been given enough attention in connection with the poet and his writings.

Calendars such as those mentioned in "An ABC" were arranged according to the Roman system of reckoning dates: that is, by Calends, Nones, and Ides.[4] The Calends were the first day of any month, the Nones the ninth day before the Ides (counting the Ides), and the Ides the thirteenth of months other than March, May, July, and October (then the fifteenth). The Romans had recorded dates as so many days before each of these points. The *Ecclesiale* (1199–1202)[5] of Alexander of Villa Dei shows that this system of giving dates was in fact employed by medieval authors, and there are many other examples. But it was not the prevailing usage in Chaucer's time, and late calendars, especially those in scientific works, frequently also number the days of the months consecutively in Arabic numerals. Chaucer sometimes uses the older method. In the Squire's Tale, he says (I, 42-7),

> And so bifel that whan this Cambyuskan
> Hath twenty wynter born his diademe,
> As he was wont fro yeer to yeer, I deme,
> He leet the feeste of his nativitee
> Doon cryen thurghout Sarray his citee,
> The laste Idus of March, after the yeer.

Other instances occur in *Troilus and Criseyde*. His usual method of giving dates, however, is about the same as present custom, with ordinal numbers and the months.

Except for their arrangement according to Calends, Nones, and Ides, the procession of the months and days did not differ from present tradition. But since calendars were not ordinarily issued for single years, some important features had to be calculated, not recorded. Among them was the week. Though other methods

10

had been tried, the week was calculated with the aid of hebdomadal (weekly) letters, the symbols A–G in recurring sets placed consecutively against all the days of the year, disregarding the changing of the months. The letter which stood next to the first Sunday of a year fell next to all the others as well. For this reason, it was called the dominical (Sunday) letter. In leap-years, the addition of the extra day, then added after 24 February, moved the dominical letter one place for the rest of the weeks, so that leap-years were considered to have two dominical letters.

Like the year, the dominical letter must always have been common knowledge. But to deal with calendars, one had to be able to tell for any year which letter of the first A–G series represented a Sunday. The connection must have been derived by calculation much of the time, for, though tables for finding the dates of various commemorations sometimes accompany ecclesiastical calendars, this is not usually the case. The calculation of the dominical letters which follows is valid for years before the Gregorian calendar reforms, instituted by the Council of Trent (1582) to correct inaccuracies resulting from inexact astronomical data and their computations. This calculation involves the solar cycle, a period of 28 years during which the seven hebdomadal letters, A–G, pass through all dates possible for them at the beginning of the year and return to their original position. If one knows the year of the solar cycle, he can find the dominical letter of that year. The year of the solar cycle is found by adding 9 to the date (e.g., 1400 + 9) and dividing the sum by 28. The quotient is the number of solar cycles that have elapsed since the beginning of the Christian era.[6] The remainder is the year of the cycle. If there is no remainder, the year is 28. The dominical letters shift backward each year, in the sequence G, F, E, D, C, B, A, and the first year of the solar cycle is always a leap-year, with the two dominical letters GF. To illustrate, the ninth year of the cycle would be counted as follows: GF, E, D, C, BA, G, F, E, DC. Being a leap-year, it would have the dominical letters DC.

11

The dominical letters may be involved in the date of *Troilus and Criseyde*. Chaucer says (I, 169–72),

> Among thise othere folk was Criseyda,
> In widewes habit blak; but natheles,
> Right as oure firste lettre is now an A,
> In beaute first so stood she, makeles.

John Livingston Lowes notes that the reference in line 171 to the letter *A* makes little sense read in terms of the alphabet. With regard to *now* in the same line he says,

> . . . there is nothing in the *present* state of the letter A as A, as compared with some other time than "now," which demands, for purposes of the simile, such curious explicitness of reference. On the assumption of a comparison with the letter solely as a letter, the passage seems inexplicable.[7]

Lowes recommends that line 171 be taken instead as a compliment to Anne of Bohemia, who married Richard II on 14 January, 1382, this reading based on traditional uses of royal initials as insignia and decorative monograms. He proposes that the word *now* points to a date for at least Book I of the *Troilus* soon after the young consort's coronation.[8]

Lowes' theory of the royal initial has found wide acceptance, and Robert Kilburn Root, writing with the astronomer Henry Norris Russell, has shown in his summary of scholarship on the matter that the consensus of academic opinion leans toward the period 1382–85 for the composition of the poem. Root and Russell place its completion not earlier than the spring of 1385, on the basis of the astronomical phenomenon described in Book III (624–28):

> The bente moone with hire hornes pale,
> Saturne, and Jove, in Cancro joyned were,
> That swych a reyn from heven gan avale,
> That every manner womman that was there
> Hadde of that smoky reyn a verray feere. . . .[9]

The planetary conjunction Chaucer describes corresponds with events of 1385, and this date has been strongly favored by Robinson and others as the earliest for the completion of the *Troilus*,[10] though both J. S. P. Tatlock[11] and J. J. O'Connor[12] have argued that Chaucer could have written about the planets from predictions, without actually seeing the conjunction that took place in 1385. But the case for 1385, or shortly thereafter, receives support from the fact that the dominical letter of 1385 was *A*. The calculation is as follows:

a) 1385 + 9 = 1394.

b)

$$
\begin{array}{r}
49 \\
28)\overline{1394} \\
112 \\
\hline
274 \\
252 \\
\hline
22 \text{ (year of the solar cycle).}
\end{array}
$$

c)

1 . . GF	12 . . G
2 . . E	13 . . FE
3 . . D	14 . . D
4 . . C	15 . . C
5 . . BA	16 . . B
6 . . G	17 . . AG
7 . . F	18 . . F
8 . . E	19 . . E
9 . . DC	20 . . D
10 . . B	21 . . CB
11 . . A	22 . . A

The year 22 corresponds with the dominical letter *A*. This may be nothing more than a coincidence, since there is no precedent for interpreting the expression *firste lettre* to mean dominical or Sunday letter. Nevertheless, Sunday being the first day of the week, *A* was the first letter of every week in 1385 and part of the commonplace information one had to know about the

13

date. While it is impossible to disprove Lowes' theory, Chaucer could have used line 171, "Right as oure firste lettre is now an A," to date his poem by the dominical letter. If he meant the expression as Queen Anne's initial, some obvious difficulties arise from the fact that his heroine is false to love.

The dominical letter was a useful device for keeping track of the seven days of the week in their recurring series. But because of the place of Sunday in the Church's worship it was also significant as one of the annotations by which calendars accommodated the liturgy. The Church's other commemorations were recorded (in Latin, in the genitive case) besides their dates. Easter, however, originating in the Jewish Passover, was set, not according to the Julian calendar, but according to the full moon on or immediately following the vernal equinox (21 March),[13] being the first Sunday thereafter. Easter and the commemorations related to it therefore had movable dates, which, like the dominical letters, had to be reckoned for each year. This involved lunar calculations, despite the fact that western society under Julius Caesar had officially abandoned the lunar months and their calendar of 354 days in favor of a strictly solar year.

Most necessary to the Church's liturgy were the golden numbers, probably so named because they were rubricated on early calendars. The golden numbers are a table of the new moons, which, among other uses, aided the reader in finding the date of Easter. Ecclesiastical calendars usually show them as a column of apparently jumbled Roman numerals, I–XIX, preceding the hebdomadal letters, though late calendars sometimes use Arabic numerals for the purpose. These numbers pertain to the metonic cycle. The metonic cycle is a period of 19 years after which the new moons begin to repeat on the same sequence of dates.[14] A year of the metonic cycle has its new moons on dates corresponding with those of the same year of the next cycle, though astronomers now know that there are inaccuracies involved.[15]

The calculation of the golden numbers for years before the

14

Gregorian reforms is simple enough: add 1 to the date (e.g., 1400 + 1) and divide the sum by 19. The quotient is the number of metonic cycles that have elapsed since the beginning of the Christian era; the remainder is the golden number; if there is no remainder, the year is 19, the last of the cycle. The lunations were considered for purposes of the calendar to consist alternately of 30 and 29 days. Thus, if one knew the golden number of a particular year he could find Easter: the Sunday immediately following the first full moon after the vernal equinox. These calculations manifestly pertain to an ecclesiastical, rather than an astronomical, moon. As noted already, calendars sometimes carry tables for finding the dates of movable feasts.

Together, the Church's anniversaries related to Easter and those related to Christmas make up an annual cycle of symbolic seasons, known as the *temporale*. Excluding feasts added to the calendar since Chaucer's time, the *temporale* and its related commemorations are as follows:

First–third Sunday of Advent
Ember Week of Advent
Fourth Sunday of Advent
Vigil of the Nativity (Christmas Eve)
Nativity (25 December)
Sunday within the octave of the Nativity
Circumcision (1 January)
Epiphany (26 January)
Sunday within the octave of the Epiphany
Second–sixth Sunday after the Epiphany
Septuagesima Sunday (9 weeks before Easter)
Sexagesima Sunday
Quinquagesima Sunday
Ash Wednesday (46 days before Easter)[16]
First Sunday of Lent (Quadragesima)
Ember Week of Lent
Second–fourth Sunday of Lent
Passion Sunday
Palm Sunday
Monday–Wednesday of Holy Week

15

Maundy Thursday
Good Friday
Holy Saturday
Easter Sunday
Monday–Saturday in Easter Week
First Sunday after Easter (Quasimodo or Low Sunday)
Second–fifth Sunday after Easter
Rogation Sunday (5 weeks after Easter)
Ascension (39 days after Easter)
Sunday within the octave of the Ascension
Whitsun Eve
Pentecost (Whit Sunday: 7 weeks after Easter)
Whit Monday, Tuesday
Ember Wednesday
Thursday in Whitsun Week
Ember Friday, Saturday
Trinity Sunday (8 weeks after Easter)
Corpus Christi (Thursday after Trinity Sunday)
Sunday within the octave of Corpus Christi
Fourth–seventeenth Sunday after Pentecost
Ember Week of September
Eighteenth–twenty-third Sunday after Pentecost.[17]

Interwoven with the *temporale* is the *sanctorale*, or annual
cycle of saints' days. Though the *temporale* is theoretically
more important than the *sanctorale*, nearly every day honors a
saint, if not more than one, so that the *sanctorale* frequently, in
fact nearly always, comes into conflict with it. This problem
has never been fully resolved, since the number of saints necessarily increases over the years. But the solution has always been
to assign rank to liturgical commemorations. Since the thirteenth
century, if not earlier, feasts have been classified as *simplex,*
semiduplex, and *duplex,* and various further classifications have
been introduced in later times.[18] Rank was earliest shown by
rubrication of the most important anniversaries of the year,
this being governed to a great extent by local tradition. In
Chaucer's day, however, and long before, scribes lettered liturgical annotations in codes of color, using, besides red, blue and

gold to contrast with the ordinary ink employed for simple feasts. Gold was used sometimes, though not always, to letter the most important commemorations. This is what Chaucer and his source, Deguilleville, mean by the reference to *Kalenderes enlumyned* in "An ABC." Calendars exhibit a great deal of variation in the use of color to denote liturgical rank, and the key to the scribe's system is not always apparent. For this reason, liturgical annotations cannot be studied without attention to color, a matter which places serious limitations upon their availability in print. The diagrams scholars have devised to reproduce them in type involve other difficulties, for, aside from being hard to understand, they create an erroneous image of medieval calendars.

In terms of the Church's calendar, Chaucer makes more references to the *sanctorale* than to the *temporale*. This is a reflection of the times, for it is well known that popular religion emphasized the saints. But some interesting observations about Chaucer himself can be made on the basis of his allusions to commemorations of the *temporale*. Most of these concern Sunday. The best known is probably the description of the Wife of Bath's holiday gear in the *Canterbury Tales* (General Prologue, 453–55):

> Hir coverchiefs ful fyne weren of ground;
> I dorste swere they weyeden ten pound
> That on a Sonday weren upon hir heed.

Presumably she wore these coverchiefs to church, for we are told immediately before (449–52),

> In al the parisshe wif ne was ther noon
> That to the offrynge bifore hire sholde goon;
> And if ther dide, certeyn so wrooth was she,
> That she was out of alle charitee.

This is for the most part the tone of Chaucer's other references to the Church's holy days, whether of *temporale* or of *sanctorale*.

Of Alison, the Carpenter's wife in the Miller's Tale (3307–11), he says,

> Thanne fil it thus, that to the paryssh chirche,
> Cristes owene werkes for to wirche,
> This goode wyf went on an haliday.
> Hir forheed shoon as bright as any day,
> So was it wasshen whan she leet hir werk.

Similarly he describes Symkyn and his wife in the Reeve's Tale (3951–55),

> A ful fair sighte was it upon hem two;
> On halydayes biforn hire wolde he go
> With his typet bounden aboute his heed,
> And she cam after in a gyte of reed;
> And Symkyn hadde hosen of the same.

The spirit of holiday is also with Chauntecleer in the Nun's Priest's Tale (2851–52):

> His voys was murier than the murie orgon
> On messe-dayes that in the chirche gon.

Besides Sunday, Chaucer mentions other commemorations of the *temporale:* Christmas, Lent, and Easter. The winter scene in the Franklin's Tale (1245–55) concerns Christmas, but it is a picture of yuletide festivity rather than of religion:

> Phebus wax old, and hewed lyk laton,
> That in his hoote declynacion
> Shoon as the burned gold with stremes brighte;
> But now in Capricorn adoun he lighte,
> Where as he shoon ful pale, I dar wel seyn.
> The bittre frostes, with the sleet and reyn,
> Destroyed hath the grene in every yerd.
> Janus sit by the fyr, with double berd,
> And drynketh of his bugle horn the wyn;
> Biforn hym stant brawen of the tusked swyn,
> And "Nowel" crieth every lusty man.

The same may be said of the comment in the Introduction to the Man of Law's Tale (126), "At Cristemasse myrie may ye daunce!" Chaucer's one overtly religious reference to Christmas is liturgical. The Prioress's Little Clergeon vows to learn the *Alma Redemptoris Mater* ". . . er Cristemasse be went" (Prioress's Tale: 540), as he hears the older schoolboys practicing it.

The word *Lente* occurs several times in Chaucer's works, though rarely in the liturgical sense. The Wife of Bath's references to it mean spring, not specifically the season of Quadragesima, as appears in her Prologue (543–59):

> And so bifel that ones in a Lente—
> So often tymes I to my gossyb wente,
> For evere yet I loved to be gay,
> And for to walke in March, Averill, and May,
> Fro hous to hous, to heere sondry talys—
> That Jankyn clerk, and my gossyb dame Alys,
> And I myself, into the feeldes wente.
> Myn housbonde was at Londoun al that Lente;
> I hadde the bettre leyser for to pleye,
> And for to se, and eek for to be seye
> Of lusty folk. What wiste I wher my grace
> Was shapen for to be, or in what place?
> Therfore I made my visitaciouns
> To vigilies and to processiouns,
> To prechyng eek, and to thise pilgrimages,
> To pleyes of myracles, and to mariages,
> And wered upon my gaye scarlet gytes.

The entire passage acquires a sacrilegious connotation if it be assumed that it refers only to the holy season of fast and abstinence. It probably does, in part, refer to Lent, for Alison mentions sermons, which, as Harry Bailly notes in the Prologue to the Clerk's Tale (12–14), had a special significance in that time:

> But precheth nat, as freres doon in Lente,
> To make us for oure olde synnes wepe,
> Ne that thy tale make us nat to slepe.

To guess which *vigilies* and *processiouns* Alison had in mind would serve little purpose: they may refer to a number of liturgical commemorations in Lent or afterwards. Weddings, however, could not be solemnized in Lent, and *pleyes of myracles* belonged to the later spring after Easter. Chaucer is here using the word *Lente* in the sense of "spring."[19] The only other instance of the word in Chaucer's works besides that in the Clerk's Tale which is clearly to the Church's Lent occurs in the Parson's Tale (102), but as a merely passing allusion in connection with public penance. Here, too, is a mention of Easter (551):

> And right so fareth it of rancour; whan it is ones conceyved in the hertes of som men, certein, it wol lasten peraventure from oon Estre day unto another Estre day, and moore.

The reference is to the custom of forgiving all grievances before Easter.[20] Other than those in the Parson's Tale, Chaucer's allusions to the commemorations of the *temporale* are full of humor and *joie de vivre*, not of religious solemnity.

Chaucer's references to the saints are far more numerous. The first question that arises is whether a calendar can be produced which contains a *sanctorale* corresponding with the saints mentioned in his works. While any fourteenth-century ecclesiastical calendar shows the *temporale* as he knew it, the contents of the *sanctorale* varied according to local and monastic tradition. Since the saints Chaucer mentions are often cited because they are saints of places he is talking about or because they are authorities on matters he is discussing, it is almost impossible that any calendar listing them all existed unless by coincidence, and indeed there is no practical reason to seek one. But it is entirely possible that there is some calendar with a *sanctorale* that can be associated with him personally. Identifying such a calendar would require direct testimony from the poet himself, internal evidence from his works, or, with regard to a document in question, connection with a place closely associated with his life for a long time.

Beginning with direct testimony, Chaucer says in the *Treatise on the Astrolabe* (Introduction, 78–86)—apparently written in 1391—that he expects to include in Part III (which is not extant) various tables, described as follows:

> ... diverse tables of longitudes and latitudes of sterres fixe for the Astrelabie, and tables of the declinacions of the sonne, and tables of longitudes of citees and townes; and tables as well for the governaunce of a clokke, as for to fynde the altitude meridian; and many anothir notable conclusioun after the kalenders of the reverent clerkes, Frere J. Somer and Frere N. Lenne.

John Somer and Nicholas of Lynne were astronomers of Oxford, whose calendars, with planetary tables for that latitude and longitude, effective from 1387 and 1386 respectively, were made for persons at court, including John of Gaunt and Joan, mother of Richard II.[21] But Chaucer was nearing fifty when these appeared, and they cannot be shown to have influenced his thinking about the saints, for the *sanctorale* was entirely independent of astronomical information. Any roster of saints could be copied on a calendar. Only by finding one of these calendars copied especially for Chaucer could anything be revealed on this basis about a *sanctorale* meaningful to him personally, and such a discovery is most unlikely.

Proceeding to internal evidence that might connect Chaucer with some particular *sanctorale*, this, if any, would reside in the saints' names that appear in his works. Most of these have been identified, and there is little left to explore in the area. There are many circumstances to which Chaucer's knowledge of the saints can be attributed, including his travels and his reading, which made him anything but parochial. At the same time, the Church's *sanctorale* was not entirely parochial either. Most of the saints represented on calendars were drawn from a common stock of names universally familiar—John the Baptist, the Virgin

Mary, apostles, early martyrs and confessors, and doctors of the Church—though specific rosters vary, often without apparent reason other than individual tradition. It is the pattern of this variation, along with the presence of names associated with the history of particular institutions or places, which identifies the provenience of ecclesiastical calendars.

In a study of Chaucer's saints (1952) which is now the most important work on the subject, Gordon Hall Gerould shows that most of those mentioned in the poet's works exclusive of the Parson's Tale (omitted as a translation) appear on the calendar of the famous Missal of Nicholas Lytlington, Abbot of Westminster 1362–86.[22] Not only was Nicholas Lytlington a contemporary whom Chaucer could have known: Westminster Abbey was the special church of the English kings, and Chaucer's connections at court make it inevitable that he was acquainted with its traditions. Indeed, one of the reasons for which the Lytlington Missal is prized is the fact that it contains the coronation ritual. But the relationship of so valuable a book to the saints mentioned in Chaucer's works is not likely to be that of a specific source. Its calendar is necessarily a reproduction of that normally in use at Westminster Abbey, involving both institutional traditions of the Benedictines and local traditions of both the Abbey and London.

The real significance of the Lytlington Missal with regard to Chaucer is its London provenience. Its *sanctorale* is not merely something the poet could have seen: it is connected with the place most closely linked with his life. But if one were to search for a calendar with a *sanctorale* typical of London, a Benedictine source, necessarily influenced by monastic custom, would not be the best choice, for laymen living in London belonged to the Diocese of St. Paul's and its parish churches. For that reason, Chaucerian scholarship could profit by identifying a secular calendar of London provenience of about the same date as the Lytlington Missal or earlier. Such a calendar is found in MS. 1 of St. Paul's Cathedral, a psalter belonging to the old Cathedral. It was probably copied earlier than 1386, since it contains two, rather than four, feasts of St. Paul and St. Erkenwald.[23] The calendar, which measures 26 cm. × 15 cm., occupies foll. 1–6ᵇ. Marginalia give information about the length of days and nights in London.

The calendar of St. Paul's Cathedral MS. 1 provides evidence of the saints which is as close as modern times are likely to come to a list of names which would have been familiar to a layman of Chaucer's day who lived in London and who knew it well. What literary use the poet may have made of any *sanctorale* is another matter. It involves the larger topic of his references to the saints, next to be examined for their liturgical implications.

NOTES TO CHAPTER II

[1] Deguilleville's corresponding lines read (11,001–03):

> Kalendier sont enlumine
> Et autre livre enterine
> Quant ton non les enlumine.

Ed. J. J. Stürzinger, *Le Pelerinage de Vie Humaine de Guillaume de Deguileville* (London, 1893). The poet's name and the title appear in various spellings. The French text is presented along with Chaucer's in Walter W. Skeat's *The Complete Works of Geoffrey Chaucer*, I (Oxford, 1894), 261–71.

[2] See, for example, Francis Wormald, ed., *English Kalendars before A. D. 1100*, Henry Bradshaw Soc., No. 72 (London, 1934); *English Benedictine Kalendars after A. D. 1100*, HBS., Nos. 77, 81 (London, 1939, 1946).

[3] Ecclesiastical calendars are discussed in the *Explanatory Supplement to the Astronomical Ephemeris and the American Ephemeris and Nautical Almanac* (London, 1961), pp. 420–29. The best book on the workings of medieval calendars for readers who have not studied astronomy is R. T. Hampson, *Medii Aevi*

kalendarium, 2 vols. (London, 1841). A less complete but easier study is P. W. Wilson, *The Romance of the Calendar* (New York, 1937). There are competent discussions under "Calendar" in the *Encyclopaedia Britannica,* 11th ed. (Cambridge, 1910), IV, 987–1004; and in the *Catholic Encyclopedia,* III, 158–66.

[4] For the discussion which follows, cf. Plates 1–12.

[5] Ed. and trans. L. R. Lind (Lawrence, Kans., 1958).

[6] The first year of the Christian era began on a Saturday. It had the dominical letter *B,* and it was the tenth year of the solar cycle.

[7] "The Date of Chaucer's *Troilus and Criseyde,*" *PMLA, XXIII* (1908), 287. The simile does not appear in Boccaccio (cf. *Filostrato* I, 19). Boccaccio's poem is presented, with a translation into Modern English, in the parallel-text edition by Nathaniel Edward Griffin and Arthur Beckwith Myrick, *The Filostrato of Giovanni Boccaccio* (Philadelphia, 1929).

[8] Pp. 288–99.

[9] "A Planetary Date for Chaucer's *Troilus,*" *PMLA,* XXXIX (1924), 48–9.

[10] For bibliography, see Robinson, p. 811 (col. 1).

[11] "The Date of the *Troilus:* and Minor Chauceriana," *MLN,* L (1935), 277–89.

[12] "The Astronomical Dating of Chaucer's *Troilus,*" *JEGP,* LV (1956), 556–62.

[13] The Council of Nicaea (325) fixed 21 March as the date of the vernal equinox, which is so marked on medieval ecclesiastical calendars though the date does not correspond exactly with the actual motion of the sun. For discussion, see Wilson, pp. 137ff, and *Astronomical Ephemeris Supplement,* p. 420.

[14] The cycle was reckoned as beginning in the year preceding the first of the Christian era, having its new moon 1 January.

[15] For discussion, see *Astronomical Ephemeris Supplement,* p. 420.

[16] The precise count of 40 days properly included in Lent is adjusted by the fact that the Latin Church does not include Sundays in the Lenten fast.

[17] Several feasts of saints are traditionally included in the *temporale:* Stephen (26 December), John the Evangelist (27 December), Holy Innocents (28 December), Thomas of Canterbury (29 December), Sylvester (31 December).

[18] For discussion, see F. G. Holweck, "Feasts," *CE,* VI, 23 (col. 1).

[19] See my "The Wife of Bath's Gay 'Lente'," *American Notes and Queries,* I (1963), 85–6. Arthur K. Moore, "'Somer' and 'Lenten' as Terms for Spring," *NQ,* CXCIV (1949), 82 (col. 1) says that Middle English *lenten* was no longer considered applicable to the season by the end of the fourteenth century, but he does not mention the Wife of Bath's references to *Lente.* The latest example of *lenten* in the sense of spring listed by the *NED* is of ca. 1320 (*A New English Dictionary on Historical Principles,* ed. James A. H. Murray, VI [Oxford, 1903], 201: "lenten").

[20] Rock, IV, 286–87.

[21] R. T. Gunther, *Early Science in Oxford,* II (Oxford, 1923), 60–5.

[22] Chaucer's Calendar of Saints," in *Chaucerian Essays* (Princeton), pp. 8–9. The Missal is edited by Legg, *Missale ad usum ecclesie Westmonasteriensis,* HBS, Nos. 1, 5, 12 (London, 1891, 1893, 1896). The Ms is described I, v–xii. The calendar is edited v–xvi.

[23] See above, pp. 5–6.

III. THE LITURGICAL BACKGROUND OF CHAUCER'S REFERENCES TO THE SAINTS

The Retraction, which follows the Parson's Tale, acknowledges for Chaucer what may have been a sizable amount of serious religious writing (1087–88):

> But of the translacion of Boece de Consolacione, and othere bookes of legendes of seintes, and omelies, and moralitee, and devocioun,/that thanke I oure Lord Jhesu Crist and his blisful Mooder, and alle the seintes of hevene. . . .

The unidentified *bookes of legendes of seintes* mentioned among his translations indicate that he had some interest in hagiography, stories of the saints. The authenticity of the Retraction has been questioned,[1] but this interest is confirmed by other evidence, for the *Canterbury Tales* contain a number of references to saints' stories. Two of the tales, the Second Nun's account of the martyrdom of St. Cecilia and the Prioress's miracle of the Virgin, are themselves hagiography, and the *Legend of Good Women* is presented as a book of martyrs. If Chaucer had not been interested in this kind of literature, there would not be so many traces of it in his works.

Hagiography is closely related to the liturgy, for, as the preceding discussion has shown, the saints' days or *sanctorale* formed an important part of the ecclesiastical year. There had always been concern with the lives and miracles of the heroes of Christianity and there had always been literature about them, some of which belonged to a large corpus of material used in the Church's services to commemorate their feasts. But little medieval hagiography is now received as completely historical. As a result, the term "legend," commonly applied to it in the Middle Ages, now means fiction from the past popularly accepted as history.

The *bookes of legendes of seintes* mentioned in the Retraction must have been a collection of saints' lives. Such works were variously known as legendaries, lectionaries, and martyrologies. A legendary or lectionary was originally a book containing the lessons or lections (readings) of the divine office, the principal liturgy of the canonical hours, arranged in the order of the ecclesiastical calendar.[2] Among the lessons for each day were the life and passion (death) of its saint or saints, according to the *sanctorale*. The fact that the *sanctorale* was larger than the *temporale* explains how the term "legend" (from the Latin *legenda* 'that which is to be read'), once synonymous with "lesson," came to refer specifically to the stories of the saints.

Liturgical books containing the lessons of the divine office continued to be called legendaries long after the close of the Middle Ages. But in Chaucer's time the name was also given to any volume containing accounts of the commemorations of the ecclesiastical year, regardless of whether it was intended for use in the Church's services. Again probably because the *sanctorale* was larger than the *temporale,* such books fell together with works known as martyrologies, which had originated as collections of saints' lives for liturgical use and which had found a wider purpose. All such books have been called legendaries, both in the Middle Ages and in modern times, though the Church has now abandoned the term "legendary" in favor of "martyrology" for its liturgical book of saints.[3]

A great deal has been written about the saints Chaucer mentions, about their identities, and about his motives for making references to them. The most comprehensive discussion is that of Gerould.[4] But any attempt to compile an unambiguous list of all cited by Chaucer entails many preliminary difficulties and would be of questionable value here. Some references are not directly to saints but to persons, places, conditions and things named for them. Two names, supposedly those of saints, receive

27

no confirmation either from tradition or from written evidence: "Ronyan" (Pardoner's Tale, Introduction, 310, 320) and "Madrian" (Monk's Tale, Prologue, 1892). Several are obscured by the fact that they can apply to more than one person. Chaucer's own part in all this is often less than clear, for some names are in his sources and their presence in his works is not due to originality. There may be instances of this which have escaped detection. The present discussion will be limited to the poet's references to the lives of the saints and to other allusions which appear to be derived from his knowledge of ecclesiastical calendars.

The indications that Chaucer had done more hagiography than is now extant offer light on some of his dealings with the saints. Although *bookes of legendes of seintes* are acknowledged in the Retraction, only one of his saints' lives has been preserved: the Second Nun's tale of St. Cecilia, thought to have been written ca. 1373 and later assigned to the Second Nun.[5] The Prioress's Tale is also hagiography, but not in the same sense. It belongs to a branch of that genre, known as miracles of the Virgin, tales of marvels attributed to the intercession of Mary.[6] The story has been identified with that of Hugh the Younger of Lincoln, a child saint reputedly slain in 1255 under circumstances similar to those described in the Prioress's Tale and commemorated at Lincoln 27 August.[7] But the Prioress does not offer her narrative as Hugh's story. She says (684–90),

> O yonge Hugh of Lyncoln, slayn also
> With cursed Jewes, as it is notable,
> For it is but a litel while ago,
> Preye eek for us, we synful folk unstable,
> That, of his mercy, God so merciable
> On us his grete mercy multiplie,
> For reverence of his mooder Marie. Amen.

For numerous reasons, especially because of an apparent materialism in the portrait of the narrator, the Prioress's Tale has been considered satire, despite the fact that the story is introduced by a prologue of some beauty. Since the sequence of portrait, Prologue and Tale is involved with Chaucer's treatment of the liturgy of the canonical hours, it will be discussed in a later chapter on that subject.[8]

Returning to the Second Nun's Tale, Chaucer's account of the life and martyrdom of St. Cecilia is very close to that given in the best known of all medieval legendaries, the *Legenda aurea* of Jacobus de Voragine (ca. 1255),[9] though the poet appears to have added details from other sources.[10] The Prologue, which has itself attracted controversy with regard to date and sources, is indebted to Jacobus for the etymologies of Cecilia's name (85-119). Less certain is the origin of the stanzas on idleness with which the Prologue begins (1-28). They may owe their inspiration to lines in the Introduction to the French translation of the *Legenda aurea* by Jehan de Vignay,[11] though Carleton Brown sees no verbal similarity and no specific indebtedness on Chaucer's part.[12] The poet speaks of his source in an envoy to the reader (78-84) immediately preceding the etymologies:

> Yet preye I yow that reden that I write,
> Foryeve me that I do no diligence
> This ilke storie subtilly to endite,
> For bothe have I the wordes and sentence
> Of hym that at the seintes reverence
> The storie wroot, and folwen hire legende,
> And pray yow that ye wole my work amende.

The Prologue has more specifically liturgical overtones than its relationship to the Church's *sanctorale* through the *Legenda aurea*. This is seen in the section entitled *Invocacio ad Mariam* (29-77). The theme is taken from St. Bernard's prayer to the Virgin in the final canto of Dante's "Paradiso" (xxxiii, 1-39):

> Maiden and Mother, daughter of thine own Son,
> Beyond all creatures lowly and lifted high,
> Of the Eternal Design the corner-stone!

Thou art she who did man's substance glorify
    So that its own Maker did not eschew
    Even to be made of its mortality.
Within thy womb the Love was kindled new
    By generation of whose warmth supreme
    This flower to bloom in peace eternal grew.
Here thou to us art the full noonday beam
    Of love revealed: below, to mortal sight,
    Hope, that forever springs in living stream.
Lady, thou art so great and hast such might
    That whoso crave grace, nor to thee repair,
    Their longing even without wing seeketh flight.
Thy charity doth not only him up-bear
    Who prays, but in thy bounty's large excess
    Thou oftentimes dost even forerun the prayer.
In thee is pity, in thee is tenderness,
    In thee magnificence, in thee the sum
    Of all that in creation most can bless.
Now he that from the deepest pit hath come
    Of the universe, and seen, each after each,
    The spirits as they live and have their home,
He of thy grace so much power doth beseech
    That he be enabled to uplift even higher
    His eyes, and to the Final Goodness reach.
And I who never burned with more desire
    For my own vision than for his, persist
    In prayer to thee—my prayers go forth in choir,
May they not fail!—that thou disperse all mist
    Of his mortality with prayers of thine,
    Till joy be his of that supreme acquist.
Also I implore thee, Queen who can'st incline
    All to thy will, let his affections stand
    Whole and pure after vision so divine.
The throbbings of the heart do thou command!
    See, Beatrice with how many of the blest,
    To second this my prayer, lays hand to hand.[13]

St. Bernard was especially renowned for his devotion to Mary.
Chaucer says (29–35),

And thow that flour of virgines art alle,
Of whom that Bernard list so wel to write,
To thee at my bigynnyng first I calle;
Thou confort of us wrecches, do me endite
Thy maydens deeth, that wan thurgh hire merite
The eterneel lyf, and of the feend victorie,
As man may after reden in hire storie.

He then develops six stanzas (lines 36–77) from the prayer:

Thow Mayde and Mooder, doghter of thy Sone,
Thow welle of mercy, synful soules cure,
In whom that God for bountee chees to wone,
Thow humble, and heigh over every creature,
Thow nobledest so ferforth oure nature,
That no desdeyn the Makere hadde of kynde
His Sone in blood and flessh to clothe and wynde.

Withinne the cloistre blisful of thy sydis
Took mannes shap the eterneel love and pees,
That of the tryne compas lord and gyde is,
Whom erthe and see and hevene, out of relees,
Ay heryen; and thou, Virgine wemmelees,
Baar of thy body—and dweltest mayden pure—
The Creatour of every creature.

Assembled is in thee magnificence
With mercy, goodnesse, and with swich pitee
That thou, that art the sonne of excellence
Nat oonly helpest hem that preyen thee,
But often tyme, of thy benygnytee,
Ful frely, er that men thyn help biseche,
Thou goost biforn, and art hir lyves leche.

Now help, thow meeke and blisful faire mayde,
Me, flemed wrecche, in this desert of galle;
Thynk on the womman Cananee, that sayde
That whelpes eten somme of the crommes alle
That from hir lordes table been yfalle;
And though that I, unworthy sone of Eve,
Be synful, yet accepte my bileve.

31

And, for that feith is deed withouten werkis,
So for to werken yif me wit and space,
That I be quit fro thennes that most derk is!
O thou, that art so fair and ful of grace,
Be myn advocat in that heighe place
Theras withouten ende is songe "Osanne,"
Thow Cristes mooder, doghter deere of Anne!

And of thy light my soule in prisoun lighte,
That troubled is by the contagioun
Of my body, and also by the wighte
Of erthely lust and fals affeccioun;
O havene of refut, o salvacioun
Of hem that been in sorwe and in distresse,
Now help, for to my werk I wol me dresse.

The sublimity of Dante's lines owes much to echoes of the
poetry of the liturgy, and Chaucer must have well understood
this, for his own stanzas contain echoes and paraphrases of
Marian liturgical material, some of which may have been suggested to him by other authors he had been reading.[14] Lines
43–7 of the third stanza of the *Invocacio* are freely translated
from the opening lines of a well-known hymn by Venantius
Fortunatus which occurs frequently in the liturgy of the canonical hours:

> Quem terra, pontus, æthera
> Colunt, adorant, prædicant:
> Trinam regentem machinam,
> Claustrum Mariæ bajulat.[15]

Another major indebtedness is to the *Salve Regina:*

> Salve, Regina, mater misericordiæ;
> Vita, dulcedo et spes nostra, salve.
> Ad te clamamus exsules filii Hevæ.
>
> Ad te suspiramus gementes et flentes in hac
>   lacrimarum valle.
> Eja ergo, advocata nostra,
> Illos tuos misericordes occulos ad nos converte.

Et Jesum, benedictum fructum ventris tui,
Nobis post hoc exsilium ostende.

Hail, O Queen, mother of mercy: our life,
sweetness, and hope, hail. To thee we cry,
exiled sons of Eve.

To thee we call, lamenting and weeping in this
valley of tears. O then, our advocate, turn
thy merciful eyes to us.

And reveal to us Jesus, the blessed fruit of
thy womb, after this exile.[16]

There are similarities to the *Salve Regina* in Chaucer's fifth
stanza (57–63):

Now help, thow meeke and blisful faire mayde,
Me, flemed wrecche, in this desert of galle;
. . . .
And though that I, unworthy sone of Eve,
Be synful, yet accepte my bileve.

The most complete study of these liturgical borrowings is that
of Brown, who suggests that they may be less a direct attempt
to quote from the liturgy than a reflection of something Chaucer
knew so well that its influence was almost unconscious.[17]
Scholars have long known that these indebtednesses are to the
little office of the Blessed Virgin Mary rather than to the divine
office, the major liturgy of the canonical hours, though some of
the materials overlap.[18] This is underscored not only by other
verbal similarities to the little office in Chaucer's fifth stanza
(47–9), but also by the fact that the *Salve Regina* does not
appear in the Sarum Breviary.[19]

Verbal similarity to the liturgy and paraphrase of it were
characteristic of much religious literature written in the Middle
Ages, and the liturgical allusions in the Second Nun's Prologue
would have been at once apparent to a medieval audience. It
is likely that Chaucer drew from the writing of this prologue
the idea for the liturgical paraphrases in the Prioress's Prologue

and Tale.[20] The fact that both pieces honor the Virgin Mary may well indicate that he was moved to their composition by religious devotion, but it must be remembered that he was under the necessity of producing poetry suitable to the nuns about whom he was writing.

The only other saint besides Cecilia with whose life Chaucer deals at any length is Kenelm. To him Chauntecleer refers in his discussion of dreams in the Nun's Priest's Tale (3110–21):

> Lo, in the lyf of Seint Kenelm I rede,
> That was Kenulphus sone, the noble kyng
> Of Mercenrike, how Kenelm mette a thyng.
> A lite er he was mordred, on a day,
> His mordre in his avysioun he say.
> His norice hym expowned every deel
> His sweven, and bad hym for to kepe hym weel
> For traisoun; but he nas but seven yeer oold,
> And therfore litel tale hath he toold
> Of any dreem, so hooly was his herte.
> By God! I hadde levere than my sherte
> That ye hadde rad his legende, as have I.

There is a comic element in Chauntecleer's telling, but no irreverence. The source is uncertain. The story is later found in Caxton's edition of the *Legenda aurea*, but it is not in the Latin original.[21] While Chauntecleer need not be taken literally, he does say that he has read Kenelm's legend, and his predilection for Latin has led Gerould to suggest that the reference is to John of Tynemouth's collection of lives of English saints.[22]

Chaucer makes other, briefer, mentions of saints' legends. He may have planned to include a life of St. Edward in the *Canterbury Tales,* for the Monk says in his Prologue (1966–72),

> I wol doon al my diligence,
> As fer as sowneth into honestee,
> To telle yow a tale, or two, or three.
> And if yow list to herkne hyderward,
> I wol yow seyn the lyf of Seint Edward;

> Or ellis, first, tragedies wol I telle,
> Of whiche I have an hundred in my celle.

Besides her reference to Hugh the Younger of Lincoln, the Prioress mentions St. Nicholas, said to have shown piety as an infant by abstaining from the breast on Wednesdays and Fridays (Prioress's Tale, 513–15):

> But ay, whan I remembre on this mateere,
> Seint Nicholas stant evere in my presence,
> For he so young to Crist dide reverence.[23]

Another saint to whom Chaucer makes brief biographical allusion is Mary of Egypt, an anchoress who died ca. 421.[24] Her legend is mentioned in connection with the plight of Constance in the Man of Law's Tale (II, 498–501):

> Where myghte this womman mete and drynke have
> Thre yeer and moore? how lasteth hire vitaille?
> Who fedde the Egipcien Marie in the cave,
> Or in desert? No wight but Crist, sanz faille.

The tradition that the apostle Thomas built churches in India is cited by the Friar in the Summoner's Tale (1978–80):

> Thomas, if ye wol lernen for to wirche,
> Of buyldynge up of chirches may ye fynde,
> If it be good, in Thomas lyfe of Inde.

Again, the reference implies that Chaucer knew of a written *vita*. This cannot have been in the *Legenda aurea*, for the detail in question is not mentioned by Jacobus, though he does present Thomas as a builder.[25] The familiar story of Mary Magdalene is mentioned twice, very briefly, in the Parson's Tale (501, 946), that of John the Baptist in the Pardoner's Tale (488–91). Of St. Dunstan, Archbishop of Canterbury (d. 988), the Devil, alluding to his own exploits, says in the Friar's Tale (1501–02),

> And somtyme be we servant unto man,
> As to the erchebisshop Seint Dunstan. . . .

35

The life of St. Dunstan does not appear in the *Legenda,* and Caxton, who gives the *vita,* does not show this incident.[26] There are, however, many stores of marvels connected with the life of St. Dunstan, and there are numerous medieval tales in which the Devil disguises himself as a servant and hires himself out to someone he wishes to destroy.[27] With regard to the sources of all these references to saints, it is evident that Chaucer made use of more hagiography than the *Legenda aurea* alone.

Chaucer's references to the lives of the saints are restrained and reverent. But from his experience with hagiography comes also the *Legend of Good Women,* a quasi-legendary containing stories of Cupid's saints. The poem is supposedly a project assigned to Chaucer by Alcestis as a penance for translating the *Roman de la Rose* and for writing *Troilus and Criseyde,* since he has thereby displeased the God of Love (*Prologue,* F 481–86; G 471–76):

> Thow shalt, while that thou lyvest, yer by yere,
> The moste partye of thy tyme spende
> In makyng of a glorious legende
> Of goode wymmen, maydenes and wyves,
> That weren trewe in lovyng al hire lyves;
> And telle of false men that hem bytraien. . . .[28]

Chaucer refers to the poem in the Introduction to the Man of Law's Tale (61) as the *Seintes Legende of Cupide,* and the Retraction (1085) calls it *the book of the xxv. Ladies*—indicating that the unfinished work is about half its intended size. The important thing here is the terminology. H. C. Goddard believes that "legend" means to Chaucer exactly what it means today: a fiction.[29] This, however, can hardly be the case with regard to the *Legend of Good Women,* because of the ecclesiastical vocabulary in the Prologue and the rubrics accompanying the *vitae,* which should be compared with those in the Sarum Legendary.[30] Chaucer, through Alcestis, calls the project a penance (Prologue, F 491; G 481), and the God of Love calls the French poem *an heresye ayeins my lawe* (Prologue, F 330;

G 256). Also, the God swears by his mother, *Seynt Venus* (Prologue, F 338; G 313), and Alcestis tells him that Chaucer has written "many an ympne for your halydayes" (Prologue, F 422; G 410). The incipits and explicits employ terminology typical of ecclesiastical calendars and legendaries: *Incipit legenda Cleopatrie, Martiris, Egipti regine; Explicit Legenda Cleopatre, martiris*. In one case, two martyrs appear together, as they often do in calendars: *Incipit Legenda Ysiphile et Medee, martirum*. Of the ten good women for whom legends are given, six are identified as martyrs: Cleopatra, Thisbe, Dido, Hypsipyle, Medea, and Lucrece. As the Church classifies most of its female saints as virgins and widows, Alcestis categorizes Love's as *maydenes and wyves* (Prologue, F 484; G 474). In short, the form and the vocabulary of the *Legend of Good Women* are too obviously ecclesiastical for Chaucer to have meant legend in any other sense. Tatlock accurately describes the poem as primarily ecclesiastical-liturgical rather than love-allegorical in its broadest conception as well as in much of the detail.[31]

The *Legend of Good Women* is revoked in the Retraction (1083–86):

> Wherfore I biseke yow mekely, for the mercy of God, that ye preye for me that Crist have mercy on me and foryeve me my giltes;/and namely of my translacions and enditynges of worldly vanitees, the whiche I revoke in my retracciouns:/as is the book of Troilus; the book also of Fame; the book of the xxv. Ladies; the book of the Duchesse; the book of Seint Valentynes day of the Parlement of Briddes; the tales of Caunterbury, thilke that sownen into synne . . . that Crist for his grete mercy foryeve me the synne.

Nevertheless, the *Legend* was more probably intended as a secular poem in the common literary traditions of courtly love than as a deliberate irreverence against the saints. These were, of course, sinful in the literal sense of medieval orthodoxy, though Gower wrote the *Confessio amantis* in the same traditions without visible damage to his reputation.[32] If Chaucer was, as frequently happens, drawn to religion in later life, there was every reason for him to retract all his secular and courtly poetry, even so gentle a work as the *Book of the Duchess*. But the *Legend of Good Women*, written in the mid-thirteen-eighties between the *Troilus* and most of the *Canterbury Tales*, is plainly not the work of a poet with piety uppermost in his mind.

This observation about Chaucer is confirmed by another manifestation of his experience with hagiography put to uses often less than reverent: the large number of saints' names appearing in his works as oaths.[33] These are found chiefly, as scholars have long been aware, at the ends of lines involving rimes. It happens that those which have attracted the most discussion occur in this position, including the controversial "corpus Madrian," "Ronyan," Loy and Clare. The first comes in the Prologue to the Monk's Tale, after Chaucer's own Tale of Melibee. The Host says (1891–94),

> As I am feithful man,
> And by that precious corpus Madrian,
> I hadde levere than a barel ale
> That Goodelief, my wyf, hadde herd this tale!

The second is also attributed to Bailly, whose vocabulary of oaths must have tried Chaucer's resourcefulness. In a passage introducing the Pardoner's Tale after the Physician's story of Virginia, having sworn by Nails and Blood and having blessed the Physician's chamber pots in the name of Our Lady, he says to him (309–10),

> "So moot I theen, thou art a propre man,
> And lyk a prelat, by Seint Ronyan!"

He then calls upon the Pardoner (317–20):

> "Myn herte is lost for pitee of this mayde.
> Thou beel amy, thou Pardoner," he sayde,
> "Telle us som myrthe or japes right anon."
> "It shal be doon," quod he, "by Seint Ronyon!"

The Pardoner has obviously taken his oath from the Host's words to the Physician, producing a rime with *anon* in the line above. No record of saints named Madrian or Ronyan has been found, though there are many theories on the subject of their possible identities.[34]

Perhaps even more famous than these references to Madrian and Ronyan is the oath in Chaucer's description of the Prioress in the General Prologue (118–20):

> Ther was also a Nonne, a PRIORESSE,
> That of hir smylyng was ful symple and coy;
> Hire gretteste ooth was but by Seinte Loy. . . .

Loy (Eligius or Eloy), a seventh-century bishop of Noyon, was the patron saint of workers in metal and enamel and also of carters and farriers, strange as the combination may appear. His name occurs in the latter context, also as a rime, in the Friar's Tale (1564–65):

> That was wel twight, myn owene lyard boy.
> I pray God save thee, and Seinte Loy!

Still another notable instance of saints' names in riming oaths belongs to the remarkable eagle in the *House of Fame*, who swears by so unlikely a saint as Clare when Chaucer inquires whether the noise he is hearing comes from people on earth (II, 1063–66),

> "And that there lives body nys
> In al that hous that yonder ys,
> That maketh al this loude fare."
> "Noo," quod he, "by Seynte Clare. . . ."

Now, Chaucer rarely assigns such phrases to himself when speaking as a *persona*. But neither this fact nor his statement of non-responsibility for the rude speech of some of his characters explains these rimed oaths as something he needed and used strictly for purposes of realism. He says in the General Prologue (725–36),

> But first I pray yow, of youre curteisye,
> That ye n'arette it nat my vileynye,
> Thogh that I pleynly speke in this mateere,
> To telle yow hir wordes and hir cheere,
> Ne thogh I speke hir wordes proprely.
> For this ye knowen al so wel as I,
> Whoso shal telle a tale after a man,
> He moot reherce as ny as evere he kan
> Everich a word, if it be in his charge,
> Al speke he never so rudeliche and large,
> Or ellis he moot telle his tale untrewe,
> Or feyne thyng, or fynde wordes newe.

Perhaps Chaucer did have specific motives for mentioning "Madrian," "Ronyan," Loy (Eligius), and Clare in the contexts that have been noted. Reasons are sometimes obvious in his oaths by saints' names, as, for example, when the Oxford carpenter in the Miller's Tale swears by St. Frydeswyde (3449), patron saint of his town. But this need not be the case in every instance, and scholars, who have written voluminously on the subject, may have wasted much effort seeking particular motives that do not exist. While Gerould has insisted that Chaucer was too adept a craftsman to go hunting for a rime,[35] it is likely that no one composing rimed verse is entirely spared such necessity. Oaths by saints' names occur in rimes too often in Chaucer's works not to have much of their explanation in the exigencies of versification.

Precisely how the idea of using riming oaths by saints' names came to Chaucer's attention it is impossible to say. The device may have been, like the riming proverb, a manner of speaking in that day. But the fund of names involved is something else. Certainly, anyone who had translated *bookes of legendes of seintes,* as the Retraction claims, would have been conversant with the lore of hagiography. But more than that, Chaucer was a government official who had many occasions to use calendars. That he was interested in the workings of the calendar *per se* the *Treatise on the Astrolabe* is eventually as strong testimony as could be desired. There is every reason to suppose that his experience in hagiography accounts for many of the saints' names that occur in his works, and it is entirely within the order of probability that he used the *sanctorale* of one or more calendars as a thesaurus of rimes. Nor is such an observation in any sense iconoclastic with regard to Chaucer's genius, for he produced in this manner of writing some of the most famous lines in English literature.

NOTES TO CHAPTER III

[1] For discussion and bibliography regarding the authenticity of the Retraction, see Robinson, p. 772 (col. 2).

[2] See, for example, the printed edition of the Sarum Legendary, *Legende totius anni tam de tempore quam de sanctis secundum ordinem Sarisburiensis* (Paris, 1518): described by A. W. Pollard and G. R. Redgrave, *A Short-Title Catalogue of Books Printed in England, Scotland, & Ireland And of English Books Printed Abroad 1475–1640* (London, 1926), p. 363 (col. 1), no. 16137. The best historical studies of medieval hagiography for students of literature are Hippolyte Delehaye, *The Legends of the Saints*, trans. Donald Attwater (New York, 1962); and Gerould, *Saints' Legends* (Boston and New York), 1916.

[3] The present Roman Martyrology was issued in 1583. The edition of 1584, approved by Gregory XIII, was officially adopted for the Church.

[4] "Chaucer's Calendar of Saints."

[5] Robinson, p. 755 (col. 2).

[6] See my *The Middle English Miracles of the Virgin* (San Marino, Calif., 1964), pp. 3–10.

[7] For discussion of the sources regarding Hugh the Younger, see J. W. F. Hill, *Medieval Lincoln* (Cambridge, 1948), pp. 223–38.

[8] See below, pp. 60–75.

[9] Ed. Theodore Graesse, 2nd ed. (Leipzig, 1850), pp. 771–77. Discussion and bibliography concerning the date, which is controversial, are given by Minnie E. Wells, "The *South English Legendary* in Its Relation to the *Legenda Aurea*," *PMLA*, LI (1936), 337–40. The *Legenda aurea* is translated by Granger Ryan and Helmut Ripperger, *The Golden Legend*, 2 vols. (London, 1941); the story of St. Cecilia appears II, 689–95.

[10] For discussion and summary, see Tatlock, "Chaucer and the *Legenda Aurea*," *MLN*, XLV (1930), 296–98.

[11] A parallel-text edition of the legend of St. Cecilia according to Jacobus de Voragine and Jehan de Vignay is given by F. J. Furnivall, Edmund Brock, and W. A. Clouston, *Originals and Analogues of Some of Chaucer's Canterbury Tales*, Chaucer Soc., 2nd Ser., No. 10 (London, 1875), pp. 192–205. Jehan de Vignay's Idleness Prologue is edited pp. 190–91. The French work was printed by Antoine Vérard. A copy of the edition of 1493 is in the Library of Congress (Rosenwald Collection).

[12] "The Prologue of Chaucer's 'Lyf of Seint Cecilie'," *MP*, IX (1911), 1–16.

[13] Trans. Laurence Binyon, *The Divine Comedy*, in *The Portable Dante*, ed. Paolo Milano (New York, 1947).

[14] Lowes, "The Second Nun's Prologue, Alanus, and Macrobius," *MP*, XV (1917–18), 1–10.

[15] Francis Procter and Christopher Wordsworth, eds., *Breviarium ad usum insignis ecclesie Sarum*, II (Cambridge, 1879), col. 286. For a modern edition and history of the hymn, see Matthew Britt, O.S.B., *The Hymns of the Breviary and Missal*, 2nd ed. revised (New York, 1955), pp. 349–51.

[16] Britt, pp. 67–8 (the translation is mine). A last line, "O clemens, O pia, O dulcis Virgo Maria," found in modern texts, is not proper to medieval texts except in the form of versicles and responses, which are sometimes very elaborate: cf. Henry

Littlehales, ed., *The Prymer or Lay Folks' Prayer Book,* Early English Text Soc., O. S., No. 109, (London, 1897), pp. lviii–lix.

[17] P. 12.

[18] For bibliography, see Robinson, p. 756.

[19] Procter and Wordsworth, I (1882), II (1879), III (1886). The liturgy of the canonical hours and its books are discussed below, pp. 60–75.

[20] Robert A. Pratt, "Chaucer's Borrowing from Himself," *MLQ,* VII (1946), 259–61.

[21] Edited by F. S. Ellis, *The Golden Legend; or, Lives of the Saints as Englished by William Caxton* (London, 1900), IV, 60–6.

[22] "Chaucer's Calendar of Saints," p. 18. The book was revised in the fifteenth century, probably by John Capgrave, and printed by Wynkyn de Worde (1516) under the title *Nova legenda Anglie:* ed. Carl Horstmann, 2 vols. (Oxford, 1901). Kenelm's legend appears II, 110–13.

[23] Ryan and Ripperger, I, 17; Graesse, 22.

[24] Ryan and Ripperger, I, 229; Graesse, 247–49.

[25] Ryan and Ripperger, I, 39–46; Graesse, 32–9.

[26] Ellis, III, 188–92.

[27] Stith Thompson, *The Folktale* (New York, 1951), p. 43. A notable example is the case of Brother Rush, who takes service in a monastery. See William J. Thoms, *Early English Prose Romances* (New York, 1907), pp. 409–40; and W. D. Paden, "Jacques de Vitry, the Mensa Philosophica, Hödeken, and Tennyson," *Journal of American Folklore,* LVIII (1945), 44, n. 32.

[28] All quotations from the Prologue are from the *F*-Version and are accompanied by the numbers of the corresponding lines in the *G*-Version. For discussion and bibliography concerning the relative merits and order of composition of the two versions, see Robinson, pp. 839–40.

[29] "Chaucer's Legend of Good Women," *JEGP*, VIII (1909), 56–7.

[30] See above, n. 2.

[31] "The Source of the Legend, and Other Chauceriana," *SP*, XVIII (1921), 421–22, n. 7.

[32] Ed. Reinhold Pauli, 3 vols. (London, 1857).

[33] See Yuzaburo Murata, "The Swearings in Chaucer," *Studies in English Grammar and Linguistics* (Otsuka Festschrift), Tokyo, 1958, pp. 289–99.

[34] For bibliography, see Robinson, p. 64, n. 120; and Gerould, "Chaucer's Calendar of Saints," pp. 14–16.

[35] "Chaucer's Calendar of Saints," p. 30.

IV. CHAUCER AND THE LITURGY OF THE
SACRAMENTS

The poet who dealt thus with the ecclesiastical year and its saints has less to say about the religious pageantry associated with the Middle Ages than might be expected of an author who wrote so much about the contemporary scene. If indeed he sometimes mentions the Church's ceremonies, he rarely gives description, though pagan rites appear in his imaginary world of Greece and Troy. This is nowhere more visible than in his treatment of the ceremonies of the sacraments, which brought the liturgy closest to the lives of the people. As a man of his time, Chaucer must have received most of the sacraments himself, and his approach to this aspect of the liturgy should reveal something about him as a person.

An exploration of this dimension of Chaucer's religious outlook is closely involved with other matters, not the least of which is the controversial problem of his relationship to Wyclif. He has been thought fundamentally unconcerned with the religious issues of the day by an impressive roster of those who have contributed to the critical literature on his works: among others, Thomas R. Lounsbury (1892),[1] Robert Kilburn Root (1906),[2] G. G. Coulton (1909),[3] Tatlock (1916),[4] John Edwin Wells (1916),[5] Aldous Huxley (1927),[6] and Eleanor Carroll Chilton (1929).[7] Tatlock described him as a "Laodicean."[8] This idea is no longer as prevalent as it used to be. Without seeing Chaucer as a direct participant in Wyclif's movement, Roger S. Loomis demonstrated (1940) that his works not only show sympathy with many Wycliffite criticisms of the Church in that society, but also in some cases echo cliché expressions characteristic of Lollard writings.[9] The main stream of controversy in this area since 1940 has not been the extent to which Chaucer was aloof from contemporary religious issues but the extent to which he was committed to Wyclif's teachings.

As Loomis has observed, Chaucer's stipends from three orthodox but far from immaculate kings, his love allegories, and his racy fabliaux hardly present him as a zealot or as a reformer.[10] Nor, it may be added, do his facile use of saints' names as oaths and his interest in the worldly aspects of the Church's calendar. But it is well known that Chaucer had a conscience with regard to some of the problems which then beset the Church. This is plainly shown in his portrait of the ideal Parson, long the focal point of academic debate on the whole question of his relationship to Wyclif.[11]

While not many scholars who have written about the Parson accept Doris V. Ives' opinion that the portrait is meant to represent Wyclif himself,[12] there can be no reasonable doubt that some of Chaucer's comments coincide with Lollard teachings, not all of which were heretical or completely so. Of particular concern to the present study is a statement about the Parson that reveals Chaucer as a man who favored simplicity in religion (General Prologue, 525–28):

> He waited after no pompe and reverence,
> Ne maked him a spiced conscience,
> But Cristes loore and his apostles twelve
> He taughte, but first he folwed it hymselve.

Loomis has already shown that line 527 is expressed in the very idiom of Wycliffite literature.[13] Lines 527–28 refer to preaching and to Christian example. They contrast with *pompe and reverence* and *spiced conscience* in the preceding lines. But what did these two expressions mean to Chaucer? Robinson interprets line 525, "He demanded no reverence." This appears to mean that the Parson expected no special treatment because of his clerical estate. He (Robinson) takes *spiced* in the next line as follows:

> . . . seasoned, hence highly refined, overscrupulous; possibly with the suggestion that he was not sophisticated,

46

versed in anise and cummin, and negligent of weightier
matters. Hinckley's interpretation, "unctuous, over com-
plaisant" seems less appropriate. The Parson was reasonable and not too fastidious in his dealings with his flock.
The phrase occurs again in *WB Prol*, III, 435. Skeat's
derivation of *spiced* from Fr. "espices," fees or dues
paid to a judge, is improbable.[14]

Hinckley would have been better represented by his own con-
cluding remarks:

Then vv. 525 and 526 stand in clear and clean antithesis
one to another: "He did not pompously exact defer-
ence from others, neither did he lay flattering unctions
to their souls;" "he was neither a snob nor a toady."[15]

But the Lollard vocabulary in the passage suggests that this
part of the Parson's portrait be read against Wyclif's denunci-
ation of the Sarum Ordinal in "Of Feigned Contemplative
Life."[16] Line 527 more probably means exactly what it says and
applies to the Use of Sarum, while line 528 means that the
Parson would not quibble over minutiae with regard to ceremonial at the expense of his other priestly responsibilities in
the manner described by Wyclif. The implication is that Chaucer
did not like the current emphasis upon ritual that accompanied
the widespread adoption of the Use of Sarum. This observation
receives confirmation elsewhere, and the pages which follow
will examine Chaucer's references to the ceremonies of the
sacraments in order to show how he treats ritual.

Catholicism defines a sacrament as an outward sign instituted
by Christ to give grace.[17] Chaucer's treatment of the ceremonies
involved is most conveniently discussed in the order in which
the sacraments are administered to the individual. Baptism
therefore comes first in the present study, though the poet has
actually very little to say about its ritual.[18] There is a brief
theological mention of it in connection with the forgiveness of
sins in the Parson's Tale (95–100), and there are several allusions to it in the Second Nun's Tale (217; 299–301; 379–80).

47

But Chaucer's only descriptive references are in the Man of Law's Tale. The Sultan of Syria, it will be remembered, has heard of the beauty of Constance, the daughter of the Emperor of Rome, and has decided to receive baptism, along with his entire baronage, in order to marry her. The Sultan's mother, however, has other ideas (I, 351–57):

> We shul first feyne us cristendom to take,—
> Coold water shal nat greve us but a lite!
> And I shal swich a feeste and revel make
> That, as I trowe, I shal the Sowdan quite.
> For thogh his wyf be cristned never so white,
> She shal have nede to wasshe awey the rede,
> Thogh she a font-ful water with hire lede.

She agrees to receive Christianity, and offers to give a feast after the Christening, planning all the while to have the new converts murdered. But Chaucer avoids describing the ceremony, and dismisses the rest with *occupatio* (II, 428–31):

> For shortly for to tellen, at o word,
> The Sowdan and the Cristen everichone
> Been al tohewe and stiked at the bord,
> But it were oonly dame Custance allone.

Soon Constance is adrift on the sea in a rudderless ship.

There is another reference to the ritual of baptism later on in the Man of Law's Tale, when Constance, now a queen in Northumberland, gives birth to a child (II, 722–23):

> The tyme is come a knave child she beer;
> Mauricius at the fontstoon they hym calle.

Twice in the Man of Law's Tale Chaucer has given himself opportunity to describe ceremony, and twice he has chosen not to do so.

There is no explicit reference to the sacrament of confirmation in Chaucer's works, though Cyril A. Reilly has suggested that there is an allusion to it in the Second Nun's Tale (349–53):

> And after this, Tiburce in good entente
> With Valerian to Pope Urban he wente,
>
> That thanked God, and with glad herte and light
> He cristned hym, and made hym in that place
> Parfit in his lernynge, Goddes knyght.[19]

The ritual of the sacrament of penance, however, Chaucer cites
several times, though it involves little except the penitent's act
of contrition and the confessor's absolution. There is an anach-
ronistic reference to the former in *Troilus and Criseyde* (I,
932–38), when Pandarus gives instruction to the protagonist,
who has fallen in love:

> "Now bet thi brest, and sey to God of Love,
> 'Thy grace, lord, for now I me repente,
> If I mysspak, for now myself I love.'
> Thus sey with al thyn herte in good entente."
> Quod Troilus, "A, Lord! I me consente,
> And preye to the my japes thow foryive,
> And I shal nevere more whyle I live."

It was customary to beat the breast at the words *mea culpa* in
the *Confiteor*, the liturgical act of contrition:

> Confiteor Deo, beatæ Mariæ, omnibus sanctis [et
> tibi Pater]: quia peccavi nimis cogitatione, locutione,
> et opere mea culpa: precor sanctam Mariam, omnes
> sanctos Dei [et te Pater], orare pro me.[20]

The expression *mea culpa* was often used out of context, and
a penitent could gain absolution with any words that expressed
contrition, provided, of course, that he was of the proper dispo-
sition and that he afterwards performed the penance assigned
by the confessor. Pandarus, describing to Criseyde Troilus'
confession to the God of Love, makes the anachronism a second
time (II, 519–25):

Tho gan I stalke hym softely byhynde,
And sikirly, the soothe for to seyne,
As I kan clepe ayein now to my mynde,
Right thus to Love he gan hym for to pleyne:
He seyde, "Lord, have routhe upon my peyne,
Al have I ben rebell in myn entente;
Now, *mea culpa,* lord, I me repente!"

These passages are of a piece with the *Legend of Good Women.*
With their religion of love they belong to the literary traditions
of *amour courtois.*

Chaucer's most extensive moral treatment of penance as a
sacrament is the Parson's Tale, a discourse on sin and repen-
tance translated from Raymund of Pennaforte's *Summa casuum
poenitentiae* and Guilielmus Peraldus's *Summa seu tractatus de
viciis* through some intermediate source.[21] He also has much to
say about the subject by the implications of the behavior of the
hypocritical Pardoner. But only once does the poet make direct
reference to liturgical aspects of the sacrament in this connection. The friars, who specialized in stirring the public to con-
fess their sins, were noted for making the matter as easy as
possible. Chaucer says of his Friar in the General Prologue
(221-24),

Ful swetely herde he confessioun,
And plesaunt was his absolucioun:
He was an esy man to yeve penaunce,
Ther as he wiste to have a good pitaunce.

The three liturgical references to penance that have been described clearly have their explanation in reasons other than
interest in ritual: those in the *Troilus* belong to courtly tradition, and that in the General Prologue is a detail necessary to
Chaucer's portrayal of a particular type of rogue.

While baptism and penance were a familiar part of life in
the Middle Ages, the liturgy of the eucharist, the mass, was far
more visibly a feature of the everyday scene. So called from

the words, *Ite, missa est,* which accompany its final benediction, the mass was celebrated daily, often more than once, and the people were required to attend it on Sundays and on certain feasts. It was customary to hallow important occasions with the mass, and no one born into that society could fail to be influenced by its constant presence in the world in which he lived.

The mass then as now consisted of a framework, called the ordinary, built around the canon or consecration ritual—which differed among the derived rites only in minutiae of ceremonial. Into this framework was inserted variable material, called the proper, according to the commemorations of the *temporale* and *sanctorale:* introit, collects, epistle, gospel, offertory, secret, communion, and post communion. All uses had special ceremonies for masses of particular occasions, such as Holy Week, matrimony, and burial of the dead. As stated earlier in the present study the mass according to the Use of Sarum differed from that of other English uses in the employment of more ritual.[22]

References to the mass are more numerous in Chaucer's works than references to ceremonies of the Church's other sacraments. They cover a variety of occasions. Mass is said for the Little Clergeon in the Prioress's Tale (635–41):

> Upon this beere ay lith this innocent
> Biforn the chief auter, whil masse laste;
> And after that, the abbot with his covent
> Han sped hem for to burien hym ful faste;
> And whan they hooly water on hym caste,
> Yet spak this child, whan spreynd was hooly water,
> And song *O Alma redemptoris mater!*

Although in modern times the *Requiem,* or special mass for the dead, need not be the funeral mass for a young child, there is evidence that this was the case in the Middle Ages.[23] Lines 637–41 refer to the blessing with holy water in the burial ritual which followed the *Requiem* before the corpse was taken from the church.[24] This passage is as close as Chaucer ever comes to describing the burial services, though he several times alludes to funeral processions (cf. the Wife of Bath's Prologue, 593–602).

The mass is also mentioned in a reference to a marriage custom in the Merchant's Tale (1885–96):

> The moone, that at noon was thilke day
> That Januarie hath wedded fresshe May
> In two of Tawr, was into Cancre glyden;
> So longe hath Mayus in hir chambre abyden,
> As custume is unto thise nobles alle.
> A bryde shal nat eten in the halle
> Til dayes foure, or thre dayes atte leeste,
> Ypassed been; thanne lat hire go to feeste.
> The fourthe day compleet fro noon to noon,
> Whan that the heighe masse was ydoon,
> In halle sit this Januarie and May,
> As fressh as is the brighte someres day.

But rarely does Chaucer show ceremonial. Medieval fabliaux often treat the mass, as other aspects of religion, with levity, and Chaucer's are no exception. One such instance concerns the foolishness of Absolon in the Miller's Tale (3339–42):

> This Absolon, that jolif was and gay,
> Gooth with a sencer on the haliday,
> Sensynge the wyves of the parisshe faste;
> And many a lovely look on hem he caste. . . .

There is another in the Shipman's Tale. The monk Dan John has to say mass because he is a priest, and he is obliged to fast before he does so. Thus, when the Merchant of Saint-Denis goes early to work upon his accounts, his wife says (220–23),

> Com doun to-day, and lat youre bagges stonde.
> Ne be ye nat ashamed that daun John
> Shal fasting al this day alenge goon?
> What! lat us heere a messe, and go we dyne.

It is not lost upon the reader that this Dan John and the Merchant's wife have just stolen an embrace. But Chaucer is writing a fabliau, and he continues (251–54),

> But hastily a messe was ther seyd,
> And spedily the tables were yleyd,
> And to the dyner faste they hem spedde,
> And richely this monk the chapman fedde.

The aspect of the mass which Chaucer singles out most frequently for comment is the offertory. The first such reference is his famous remark about the Wife of Bath in the General Prologue (449–52):

> In al the parisshe wif ne was ther noon
> That to the offrynge bifore hire sholde goon;
> And if ther dide, certeyn so wrooth was she,
> That she was out of alle charitee.

The offertory procession was a familiar custom in the Middle Ages, and the Parson's Tale has an admonition on the subject (406):

> And yet is ther a privee spece of Pride, that waiteth first to be salewed er he wole salewe, al be he lasse worth that that oother is, peraventure; and eek he waiteth or desireth to sitte, or elles to goon above hym in the wey, or kisse pax, or been encensed, or goon to offryng biforn his neighebor. . . .[25]

The Wife of Bath's foibles in this direction are presented in a spirit of good humor, and Chaucer is obviously laughing at the ridiculous Absolon in the Miller's Tale (3348–51):

> This parissh clerk, this joly Absolon,
> Hath in his herte swich a love-longynge
> That of no wyf took he noon offrynge;
> For curteisie, he seyde, he wolde noon.

The poet also singles out the offertory in his portrait of the Pardoner in the General Prologue (709–14):

> Wel koude he rede a lessoun or a storie,
> But alderbest he song an offertorie;
> For wel he wiste, whan that song was songe,
> He moste preche and wel affile his tonge
> To wynne silver, as he ful wel koude;
> Therfore he song the murierly and loude.

Maskell notes that the sermon was preached after the gospel, after the creed, or after the offertory.[26] The Pardoner's own Prologue well summarizes his situation (400–02):

> Of avarice and of swich cursednesse
> Is al my prechyng, for to make hem free
> To yeven hir pens, and namely unto me.

In a similar comment, the Friar's Tale says of the Archdeacon (1315–18),

> For smale tithes and for smal offrynge
> He made the peple pitously to synge.
> For er the bisshop caughte hem with his hook,
> They weren in the erchedeknes book.

The graft that had crept into the Church's economics was much on Chaucer's mind, and his remarks, though written with humor, are in reality intensely serious. To summarize, Chaucer's references to the mass sometimes touch on liturgical details but they do not describe.

The last sacrament with which Chaucer is concerned is matrimony.[27] Discussion of the sacrament and the institution of marriage is, as it is well known, frequent in his works and the subject of several of the *Canterbury Tales.* Chaucer's most famous remark on matrimony is liturgical. He says of the Wife of Bath in the General Prologue (460–62),

> Housbondes at chirce dore she hadde fyve,
> Withouten oother compaignye in youthe,—
> But therof nedeth nat to speke as nowthe.

The sacrament could not be repeated while both spouses lived, and Dame Alison's autobiography, which occupies a large part of her Prologue, accounts for the circumstances that have left her so often a widow.

The customs involved in a marriage ceremony in medieval England were partly social traditions and partly liturgy. The bride, if a maiden, was adorned for the occasion with a wreath of jewels or flowers upon her head, and her hair was unbound to hang loosely down her back. So Chaucer prepares Griselda for her wedding in the Clerk's Tale (II, 379–85):

> Hir heris han they kembd, that lay untressed
> Ful rudely, and with hir fyngres smale
> A corone on hire heed they han ydressed,
> And sette hire ful of nowches grete and smale.
> Of hire array what sholde I make a tale?
> Unnethe the peple hir knew for hire fairnesse,
> Whan she translated was in swich richesse.

The ceremony itself took place at the "people's door" of the church, which, according to Rock, had a wide shelter for that reason.[28] Chaucer does not tell anything of the ritual in Griselda's wedding, except (II, 386–87):

> This markys hath hire spoused with a ryng
> Broght for the same cause. . . .

He gives details, however, in his account of the marriage of January and May in the Merchant's Tale (1700–08):

> But finally ycomen is the day
> That to the chirche bothe be they went
> For to receyve the hooly sacrement.
> Forth comth the preest, with stole aboute his nekke,

And bad hire be lyk Sarra and Rebekke
In wysdom and in trouthe of mariage;
And seyde his orisons, as is usage,
And croucheth hem, and bad God sholde hem blesse,
And made al siker ynogh with hoolynesse.

The expression *hoolynesse* means "religion." Actually, Chaucer
has run together details from the marriage ceremony and the
nuptial mass which followed it. A passage in a collect from the
latter is the source of the reference to Sara and Rebecca (1704):

> Deus per quem mulier iungitur viro, et societas princi-
> paliter ordinata, ea benediccione donatur, que sola nec
> per originalis peccati penam, nec per diluvii est ablata
> sentenciam: respice propicius super hanc famulam
> tuam, que maritali iungenda est consorcio, tua se expetit
> protectione muniri. Sit in ea iugum dileccionis et pacis:
> fidelis et casta nubat in Christo, imitatrixque sanctarum
> permaneat feminarum. Sit amabilis ut Rachel viro,
> sapiens ut Rebecca, longeva et fidelis ut Sara. . . .

> O God, by Whom woman is joined to man, and that
> alliance which Thou didst ordain from the beginning
> is endowed with a blessing, which alone was not taken
> away, either in punishment of original sin or by the
> sentence of the flood, look down in mercy upon this
> Thy handmaid who, being about to enter upon wedded
> life, seeks to be strengthened by Thy protection; may
> the yoke she has to bear be one of love and peace;
> true and chaste may she marry in Christ, and be a
> follower of holy women; may she be pleasing to her
> husband like Rachel; prudent like Rebecca; longlived
> and faithful like Sara. . . .[29]

The poet concludes the ceremonial aspect of January's wedding
with the blessing of the marriage bed (1819), which he does
not describe.

Some generalizations may now be made about Chaucer's
treatment of the liturgy of the sacraments. First of all, his

business is with the living. He has little to say about death and burial. Second, he is concerned with adult life only. Though he must have witnessed infant baptism, he has almost nothing to say about its ceremonies when the subject is mentioned. Third, his liturgical references to the sacrament of penance show both his commitment to the literary traditions of *amour courtois* with its religion of love and his concern about the corruption of clerics in obtaining money from penitents. The jingle of coins also motivates his references to the offertory of the mass, though his comments about the Wife of Bath's offertory procession and about Absolon's reluctance to collect offerings from women are more humorous than anything else. His most detailed descriptions belong to the ceremonies of marriage, and they are found in one of his fabliaux. Certainly, Chaucer gave himself ample opportunity to describe ceremonial in writing about the sacraments. His references to them show that he was not interested in ritual.

NOTES TO CHAPTER IV

[1] *Studies in Chaucer* (New York), II, 469–73.

[2] *The Poetry of Chaucer* (Boston), pp. 28–31.

[3] *Chaucer and His England* (London), pp. 10–11.

[4] "Chaucer and Wyclif," *MP*, XIV, 67.

[5] *A Manual of Writings in Middle English 1050–1400* (New Haven), pp. 602–03.

[6] *Essays New and Old* (New York), p. 252.

[7] Eleanor Carroll Chilton and Herbert Agar, *The Garment of Praise* (Garden City, N. Y.), pp. 121–22.

[8] *Loc. cit.*

[9] "Was Chaucer a Laodicean?" *Essays and Studies in Honor of Carleton Brown* (New York), pp. 131–48.

[10] P. 129.

[11] Summarized by Robinson, pp. 663 (col. 2)–664 (col. 1).

[12] "'A Man of Religion'," *MLR*, XXVII (1932), 144–48.

[13] Pp. 142–43.

[14] P. 664 (col. 2); see also Skeat, V, 47.

[15] Henry Barrett Hinckley, *Notes on Chaucer* (Northampton, Mass., 1907), p. 40.

[16] See above, pp. 4–5.

[17] *The Catholic Encyclopedia*, XIII, 295 (col. 1).

[18] The ritual of baptism according to the Use of Sarum is edited by Legg, *The Sarum Missal*, pp. 130–31; and by Maskell, *Monumenta ritualia ecclesiae Anglicanae*, I (London, 1846), 22–32 (with commentary).

[19] "Chaucer's Second Nun's Tale: Tiburce's Visit to Pope Urban," *MLN*, LXIX, 37–9. For ritual, see Legg, *The Sarum Missal*, p. 131; and Maskell, *Monumenta*, I, 34–6.

[20] Maskell, *The Ancient Liturgy of the Church of England*, p. 14. The exact wording differs among English uses and even among books according to Sarum Use. Legg (*The Sarum Missal*, p. 216) gives only the rubric *Confiteor deo celi*, which agrees with the translation given by Maskell, *Monumenta*, II, 282. The *Confiteor*, being common knowledge, rarely appears in full in medieval service books.

[21] For bibliography, see Robinson, p. 766.

[22] See above, pp. 3–4.

[23] Boyd, *The Middle English Miracles of the Virgin*, p. 37. For the *Requiem*, see Legg, *The Sarum Missal*, pp. 431–45.

[24] Maskell, *Monumenta*, I, 117.

[25] The history of the offertory procession is discussed by Maskell, *The Ancient Liturgy of the Church of England*, pp. 78–81, n. 75.

[26] *The Ancient Liturgy of the Church of England*, pp. 70–3, n. 67.

[27] The ritual is given by Legg, *The Sarum Missal*, pp. 413–18; and Maskell, *Monumenta*, I, 42–64.

[28] Rock, IV, 200.

[29] Legg, *The Sarum Missal*, p. 417; and Maskell, *Monumenta*, I, 57–8. There are slight differences in wording. The translation is from F. X. Lasance and Francis Augustine Walsh, O.S.B., eds., *The New Roman Missal* (New York, 1937), pp. 1450–51.

V. CHAUCER, THE PRIORESS, AND THE LITURGY
OF THE CANONICAL HOURS

In view of Chaucer's secular attitude toward the liturgical year and its saints, and in view of the indications that, without in any way condemning liturgy as such, he was unfavorably disposed toward the current trend toward ritualism, it is interesting to find that his references to another aspect of the Church's services, the liturgy of the canonical hours, are chiefly in the Prioress's sequence of portrait, Prologue and Tale, which is widely held to be satire.[1] There is much disagreement as to precisely what Chaucer intended to satirize, and it must be noted that there have been apologists for a sympathetic reading, particularly Sister M. Madeleva, whose essay "Chaucer's Nuns" attempts to justify the Prioress's courtly manners as part of conventual training and discipline.[2] But Sister Madeleva has not been able to explain away an all too obvious worldliness in the portrait, and scholars have called attention not only to this but to the violence and anti-Semitism in the Tale: in particular, E. T. Donaldson,[3] Paull F. Baum,[4] and R. J. Schoeck. In Schoeck's words, ". . . the widely circulated ritual murder legend is held up for implicit condemnation as vicious and hypocritical."[5] This view presents serious difficulties, for medieval hagiography is notoriously anti-Semitic, and a study of other miracles of the Virgin reveals numerous tales of violence and intolerance presented in contexts of proclaimed devout purpose.[6] Chaucer says nothing to indicate that he was an exception to usual medieval social attitudes. What has not been fully realized, however, is that he has given the Prioress a markedly liturgical orientation, to which, if satire was indeed his purpose, it cannot be unrelated.

Chaucer's contemporaries would have observed at once that, of all the things he says about the Prioress in the General Prologue, it is the comment in lines 122–23 to which he afterwards draws attention in her Prologue and Tale:

Ful weel she soong the service dyvyne,
Entuned in hir nose ful semely. . . .

In that day, *service dyvyne* referred to the liturgy of the canonical hours. Her Prologue contains paraphrases of it. The story which follows begins in a school where children are learning from two of its books, the primer and the antiphoner. The central character, who is supposed to be studying from the primer, is murdered for singing an antiphon (anthem), learned indirectly from the antiphoner, as he walks through a ghetto. These liturgical elements plainly link portrait, Prologue and Tale. That some of the paraphrases are found also in the mass of Holy Innocents' Day (28 December), of which the Prioress's story contains other echoes, indicates that it, too, had a part in the composition of Chaucer's famous sequence. These liturgical paraphrases must have been meant to convey something about the Prioress, and it is the belief of most scholars who have written about her portrait that lines 122–23 of the General Prologue occur in a context which is anything but spiritual. It is here proposed that Chaucer is making fun of the Prioress's liturgical orientation, which contrasts with the absence of other virtues of the religious calling such as those idealized in the portrait of the Parson.

The comment about the Prioress's *service dyvyne* in General Prologue 122–23 is the key to the matter and it is bound to confuse modern readers because, in the Roman Rite, the liturgy of the canonical hours has all but disappeared from secular life. On the surface, it seems unusual that Chaucer should observe, let alone stress, this particular detail about a nun, especially on a journey. Sister Madeleva, observing that nuns never sing office on journeys, writes,

. . . he must have been at some convent for only there could he have heard the "service divyne entuned."

> . . . One might go further and infer that through
> business or ties of kinship he must have been well
> acquainted with some community; a stranger or a casual
> visitor does not ordinarily hear the religious chanting
> the Office, or if he does, he is not able to interpret it as
> Chaucer does.[7]

But this comment is based upon modern, not medieval, custom. Statutes of secular cathedrals such as Salisbury and St. Paul's provided for the singing of the liturgy of the canonical hours in choir,[8] and countless literary allusions show laymen attending these services in churches and chapels. In *Sir Gawain and the Green Knight,* for example, Gawain, seeking to break his journey toward his appointment with the beheading stroke and its fantastic donor, searches for a place where he hopes to hear matins as well as mass (753–57):

> And therefore siking he said, "I beseche the, lord,
> And Mary, that is mildest moder so dere,
> Of sum herber there highly I might here masse,
> And thy matines to-morn, mekely I ask,
> And therto prestly I pray my Pater and Ave and crede."[9]

A company of fourteenth-century pilgrims was as likely to hear the liturgy of the canonical hours in English churches as people are to hear vespers (evensong) today, and there is no evidence that anyone was prohibited from taking part in such services who knew how to do so.[10] In creating the Prioress's sequence with its allusions to the *service dyvyne,* Chaucer was dealing with a familiar institution, not with something understood only by those who had special connections with convents. In drawing attention to her *semely* rendition of it, he might in a different context be praising virtue. But this Madame Eglentyne is notable for her sentimentality and for her manners, not for her fidelity to the ideals of religion as set forth by Chaucer in his portrait of the Parson. Her Prologue and her Tale use her liturgical orientation to show the emotionalism of her personality.

While this could not have been lost upon Chaucer's intended audience, his modern readers are another matter. The poet was not in a position to know that later generations would be unfamiliar with the liturgy of the canonical hours. Some background information is therefore important to the present discussion.

The canonical hours are intervals derived from the Roman watches, their exact times varying with the lengths of days and nights according to the seasons. These intervals, greatly modified and with the addition of compline (which is not derived from them), became the basis of monastic routine in the sixth century under St. Benedict's rule:

matins	(midnight)	sext	(to midday)
lauds	(daybreak)	none	(to 3 p.m.)
prime	(to 6 a.m.)	vespers	(to 6 p.m.)
tierce	(to 9 a.m.)	compline	(the hour of retiring)

The daylight hours were a familiar part of the idea of time in the Middle Ages, and Chaucer makes many references to them in that sense. He says of January in the Merchant's Tale (1855–57),

> Thanne seide he thus, "My reste wol I take;
> Now day is come, I may no lenger wake."
> And doun he leyde his heed, and sleep til pryme.

In the Nun's Priest's Tale (3191–97),

> Bifel that Chauntecleer in al his pryde,
> His sevene wyves walkynge by his syde,
> Caste up his eyen to the brighte sonne,
> That in the signe of Taurus hadde yronne
> Twenty degrees and oon, and somwhat moore,
> And knew by kynde, and by noon oother loore,
> That it was pryme, and crew with blisful stevene.

Bells were rung at the canonical hours. Chaucer says in the Pardoner's Tale (661–63),

> Thise riotoures thre of whiche I telle,
> Longe erst er prime rong of any belle,
> Were set hem in a taverne for to drynke. . . .

In the Miller's Tale (3655–56), he says that Alison and Nicholas stayed abed

> Til that the belle of laudes gan to rynge,
> And freres in the chauncel gonne synge.

Various series of services were associated with the canonical hours, the most important being the divine office (Lat. *officium* 'duty'), the similar but shorter little office of the Blessed Virgin Mary, and the office of the dead. Cathedral canons and regular (monastic) clergy were required to chant them in choir unless they were specifically excused. They were sometimes assisted by boys. Cathedrals and monasteries often had schools for the education of children, but it is clear from the Prioress's Tale that academic education needed not be deeply involved in the training of boy choristers, who were taught the liturgical chant when they were very young. The Little Clergeon's schoolfriend, older than his own seven years, is learning to chant from the antiphoner, but he knows little more than Latin pronunciation, for he cannot translate what he is singing. In his own words (531–36),

> This song, I have herd seye,
> Was maked of our blisful Lady free,
> Hire to salue, and eek hire for to preye
> To been oure help and socour whan we deye.
> I kan namoore expounde in this mateere;
> I lerne song, I kan but smal grammeere.

It is not known how the canonical hours and their liturgy were managed at the parish level. Some writers think that the services were portioned out among the diocesan clergy so that they were not responsible for all of them.[11]

The principal liturgy of the canonical hours is the divine office. There was in the Middle Ages no uniform text of its services universally prescribed for the Roman Rite, but it was everywhere understood to be a cycle of choir services based on the psalms and intended to cover the entire Book of Psalms at stated intervals, together with hymns, lessons (readings or lections) from the Old and New Testaments, from the fathers of the Church, and from the lives of the saints, as well as other devotional materials. While tradition imposed a degree of uniformity, the materials were adapted to various diocesan and monastic derived rites by means of their individual ordinals.[12] Numerous books were needed for these services.[13] Chaucer mentions three in addition to the Bible: the legendary, the antiphoner, and a volume which he calls *porthors*. The legendary has been discussed in connection with the *Legend of Good Women*.[14] The antiphoner was the chantbook of the divine office. Chaucer describes it as the book from which the schoolboys in the Prioress's Tale (518–19) are learning the *Alma Redemptoris Mater*. He refers to *porthors* in the Shipman's Tale (131–33), where the monk Dan John swears by his:

> For on my porthors here I make an ooth
> That nevere in my lyf, for lief ne looth,
> Ne shal I of no counseil yow biwreye.

A *porthors*, also written in various similar spellings, was any medieval antecedent of the Roman Breviary of modern times, which was first issued in the sixteenth century by Pius V. There were many attempts in the Middle Ages to introduce and popularize a one-volume portable text of the divine office, and there is no way of discovering whether Chaucer had any particular version in mind.[15] Many medieval breviaries became portable at the expense of legibility. The writing is often so small that the intended owners must have known most of the materials from memory and used their books primarily for cues.

The *porthors* or breviary is not the same as the primer, the book from which the Little Clergeon is studying in the Prioress's

Tale (516–17). The principal contents of the primer were the little office of the Blessed Virgin Mary and the office of the dead. In monastic orders, both were sung in choir as well as the divine office. Like other medieval books containing the Church's services of worship, the primer existed in numerous versions. Present-day manuscript collections contain many copies, and certain of them are famous art treasures. Also known as *horae* or books of hours (names for some reason favored by modern scholars though primer or *primarium* was equally common in the Middle Ages),[16] the primer had an additional use as a book for instructing beginners in the liturgical chant. This is the sense in which the Prioress's Tale refers to it.

The primer must have reached large numbers of people, for the clergy were bound to the little office as to the divine office until 1538, when they were dispensed by the bull of Pius V, *Quod a nobis*,[17] and the office of the dead was part of the mores regarding commemoration of the departed. James J. Rorimer is mistaken when he identifies the primer (which he calls book of hours) as intended for private prayer in contrast with official church service books,[18] though this might be said of an English translation. That some primers consist chiefly of illustrations and first lines is probably because the materials, made up mostly of psalms and hymns, were so familiar that people knew them from memory. Indeed, the use of cues instead of full texts is characteristic of medieval service books, a matter which now presents no small difficulty to scholars trying to work with them.

The contents of the primer were inevitably familiar to Chaucer. There is a possible reference to the office of the dead in the Summoner's Tale. Chaucer says (2074–76) after recounting a murder committed by Cambyses,

> Beth war, therfore, with lordes how ye pleye.
> Syngeth *Placebo*, and 'I shal, if I kan,'
> But if it be unto a povre man.

The Parson's Tale makes a similar comment (616): "Flatereres been the develes chapelleyns, that syngen evere *Placebo*."

Placebo was the common name for the vespers of the office of the dead, from Psalm 114 and the antiphon *Placebo Domino in regione vivorum,* with which the service of vespers begins.

More significant to the present study is the little office of the Blessed Virgin Mary, associated with the Prioress's Tale because Chaucer opens its famous Prologue with a paraphrase of Psalm 8, the first of three psalms which form the basis of matins (453–59):

> "O Lord, oure Lord, thy name how merveillous
> Is in this large world ysprad," quod she;
> "For nought oonly thy laude precious
> Parfourned is by men of dignitee,
> But by the mouth of children thy bountee
> Parfourned is, for on the brest soukynge
> Somtyme shewen they thyn heryinge."

The Prioress's Prologue contains other paraphrases which can be traced to the little office, though all of these materials are also found in the divine office. About this fact Sister Madeleva writes,

> Chaucer makes his excerpts, not from the Divine, but from the Little Office. The reason is easy. He was more familiar with it and knew that all the psalms and prayers it contained were included in the longer Office which the Nuns actually said.[19]

But the very overlap of materials means that this cannot be proved. The liturgical paraphrases in the Prioress's Prologue must have a better explanation for their presence than the one Sister Madeleva proposes. And indeed they do. Having commented in General Prologue 122–23 on the Prioress's preciseness with regard to the liturgy of the canonical hours, Chaucer uses that point to connect the portrait with what follows. He introduces her miracle of the Virgin with a prologue beginning with a paraphrase of the opening psalm of matins of the little office, which, as a familiar Marian devotion, was an ideal note on which to open such a tale.

Chaucer paraphrases liturgical material from at least one other source in the Prioress's Prologue and Tale. This has been seen as a controversy over origins, rather than as a development, which it more probably is. Marie P. Hamilton writes,

> . . . Psalm 8 is prominent in the Matins service, which would have been familiar to the Prioress, but in view of the various echoes of the Mass of Holy Innocents in the story itself, it is reasonable to suppose that Chaucer had in mind the Introit of the Mass in this passage.[20]

The introit, called *officium* in the Use of Sarum, is the entrance chant of the mass. Originally, it was a psalm arranged with an antiphon (usually a verse from the same psalm) and a doxology. By the late Middle Ages, the psalm was usually represented by its opening verse only, and the resulting introit followed the order antiphon, psalm verse, doxology, antiphon, thus stressing the antiphon. In some early uses and in the pontifical mass celebrated at Rome, the entire psalm was sung in the manner called *repetenda:* that is, verses of the psalm were sung in alternation with the antiphon.[21] Whatever the method, the introit stressed the antiphon, rather than the literal text of the psalm, and masses were usually named for the opening words of their introit's antiphon. At the beginning of the Prioress's Prologue, Chaucer's wording follows the psalm as it appears in the little office, rather than in the introit of the mass of Innocents' Day, which the Sarum Missal gives as follows:

> Ex ore infancium Deus et lactencium perfecisti laudem propter inimicos tuos.
>
> *Ps.* Domine dominus noster. Amen.[22]

There is other evidence that Chaucer had the little office in mind, for the Clergeon is first presented in a school where he is studying the primer, which, it will be remembered, contains the text of the little office, while the older children are learning from the antiphoner, the chant-book of the divine office. While there is a great deal of redundancy among the contents of medieval service books, Chaucer's setting plainly belongs, not to the mass of Innocents' Day as Mrs. Hamilton has thought, but to the liturgy of the canonical hours.

But Mrs. Hamilton is absolutely right when she observes that there are echoes of the mass of Innocents' Day in the Prioress's Prologue and Tale. There is every reason to believe that Chaucer intended his liturgical allusions to overlap and that he meant to convey something thereby. He works into the mass, called from its introit *Ex ore infantium,* by repeating in the Tale (607–08),

> O grete God, that parfournest thy laude
> By mouth of innocentz, lo, heere thy myght!

This, as shown above, is the *motif* of the introit, derived from Psalm viii. 2–3, and Chaucer obviously means it to represent the theme of the Little Clergeon's tragedy. His Prioress makes this point in two ways. First, she paraphrases other scriptural passages as she tells her Tale, which are unmistakably from the lesson, gospel, and communion of the same mass:

Prioress's Tale (579–85)

> O martir, sowded to virginitee,
> Now maystow syngen, folwynge evere in oon
> The white Lamb celestial—quod she—
> Of which the grete evaungelist, Seint John,
> In Pathmos wroot, which seith that they that goon
> Biforn this Lamb, and synge a song al newe,
> That nevere, flesshly, wommen they ne knewe.

Lesson (Apoc. xiv.1–5)

> In diebus illis: Vidi supra montem Syon agnum stantem . . . Sine macula sunt ante thronum Dei.

> In those days I saw upon Mount Sion a Lamb standing, and with Him a hundred forty-four thousand having His name, and the name of His Father, written

on their foreheads. And I heard a noise from heaven, as the noise of many waters, and as the voice of great thunder; and the voice which I heard was as the voice of harpers, harping on their harps. And they sung as it were a new canticle, before the throne, and before the four living creatures, and the ancients; and no man could say the canticle, but those hundred forty-four thousand who were purchased from the earth. These are they who were not defiled with women, for they are virgins. These follow the Lamb whithersoever he goeth. These were purchased from among men, the first-fruits to God and to the Lamb; and in their mouth there was found no lie; for they are without spot before the throne of God.[23]

Prioress's Tale, 625–27

> His mooder swownynge by the beere lay;
> Unnethe myghte the peple that was theere
> This newe Rachel brynge fro his beere.

Gospel (Matt. ii.13–18)

> In illo tempore: Angelus domini apparuit in sompnis
> . . . noluit consolari quia non sunt.

At that time an angel of the Lord appeared in sleep to Joseph, saying: Arise, and take the child and his mother, and fly into Egypt; and be there until I tell thee: for it will come to pass that Herod will seek the child to destroy Him. Who arose, and took the child and His mother by night, and retired into Egypt; and He was there until the death of Herod: that it might be fulfilled which the Lord spoke by the prophet, saying: Out of Egypt have I called my Son. Then Herod, perceiving that he was deluded by the wise men, was exceeding angry; and sending, killed all the men-children that were in Bethlehem, and in all the borders thereof, from two years old and under, according to the time which he had diligently inquired of the wise

men. Then was fulfilled that which was spoken by
Jeremias the prophet, saying: A voice in Rama was
heard, lamentation and great mourning; Rachel bewailing her children, and would not be comforted, because
they are not.[24]

Communion (Matt. ii.18)

Vox in Rama audita est ploratus et ululatus, Rachel
plorans filios suos noluit consolari quia non sunt.

A voice in Rama was heard, lamentation and mourning: Rachel bewailing her children: and would not be
comforted because they are not.[25]

But the Prioress makes her point in another way as well.
Early in the Tale she alludes to the infant piety of St. Nicholas
as an analogy with the Clergeon's innocent devotion to Our
Lady (509–15):

Thus hath this wydwe hir litel sone ytaught
Oure blisful Lady, Cristes mooder deere,
To worshipe ay, and he forgat it naught,
· For sely child wol alday soone leere.
But ay, whan I remembre on this mateere,
Seint Nicholas stant evere in my presence,
For he so yong to Crist dide reverence.[26]

The Prioress draws still another analogy. She concludes her
Tale by calling upon Hugh the Younger of Lincoln for his intercession (684–90):

O yonge Hugh of Lyncoln, slayn also
With cursed Jewes, as it is notable,
For it is but a litel while ago,
Preye eek for us, we synful folk unstable,
That of his mercy, God so merciable
On us his grete mercy multiplie,
For reverence of his mooder Marie. Amen.[27]

Each of these analogies—to the Holy Innocents, to St. Nicholas, and to Hugh the Younger of Lincoln—and the Tale itself, illustrates the *motif* of Psalm 8 found in both the little office and the mass of Innocents' Day: "Ex ore infancium et lactancium perfecisti laudem propter inimicos tuos." A contemporary audience would not have heard the story without perceiving this.

The fact that Chaucer presents the Prioress's sequence in liturgical language is plainly a development of General Prologue 122–23. Yet it is not a parody on the liturgy, for the liturgical materials are handled reverently, and the Prioress's traveling companions appear moved by what she has said. Where, then, is the satire, and what is Chaucer's purpose in underscoring so heavily the Prioress's liturgical thinking?

A closer look at her allusions to the children saints and at her liturgical paraphrases shows that they are highly emotional materials in their original contexts. Chaucer has already said of the Prioress in the General Prologue (142–50),

> But, for to speken of hire conscience,
> She was so charitable and so pitous
> She wolde wepe, if that she saugh a mous
> Kaught in a trappe, if it were deed or bledde.
> Of smale houndes hadde she that she fedde
> With rosted flessh, or milk and wastel-breed.
> But soore wepte she if oon of hem were deed,
> Or if men smoot it with a yerde smerte;
> And al was conscience and tendre herte.

The tale of the Little Clergeon and the Prioress's manner of telling it illustrate this sentimental side of her personality.

Nowhere in the Prioress's sequence does Chaucer condemn liturgy as such. His liturgical allusions reveal a close familiarity with the canonical hours and their services. By presenting the Prioress's Tale in liturgical language, he adds to its emotional impact and expresses it in a manner which could well be characteristic of someone of that day whose life was surrounded by the literature of religion. But in this particular case, the intent must be satire, for the portrait in the General Prologue, especially lines 142–50, shows the Prioress as worldly, sentimental, and indeed rather silly. Her preoccupation with the liturgy stresses not virtue but sentimentality, and hence is the type of hypocrisy decried by Wyclif in "Of Feigned Contemplative Life." As for Chaucer himself, his presentation of the Parson and the Prioress shows that he thought with Wyclif on this particular point.

NOTES TO CHAPTER V

[1] Alan T. Gaylord, "The Unconquered Tale of the Prioress," *Papers of the Michigan Academy of Science, Arts, and Letters,* XLVII (1962), 613–32.

[2] *Chaucer's Nuns and Other Essays* (New York, 1925), pp. 3–42; reprinted in *A Lost Language and Other Essays on Chaucer* (New York, 1951), pp. 31–60.

[3] *Chaucer's Poetry: An Anthology for the Modern Reader* (New York, 1958), pp. 932–34.

[4] *Chaucer: A Critical Appreciation* (Durham, N. C.), 1958, p. 79.

[5] "Chaucer's Prioress: Mercy and Tender Heart," in *Chaucer Criticism,* ed. Richard J. Schoeck and Jerome Taylor (Notre Dame, Ind.), 1960, I, 246.

[6] Boyd, *The Middle English Miracles of the Virgin,* pp. 38–43; 44–9; 68–87.

[7] *Chaucer's Nuns,* p. 12.

[8] Frere, *passim;* and Dugdale, p. 22.

[9] Ed. R. T. Jones, *Sir Gawain and the Grene Gome* (Natal, 1960). The standard edition is that of J. R. R. Tolkein, *Sir Gawain & the Green Knight* (Oxford, 1960).

[10] Rock, IV, 16–18.

[11] S. J. P. van Dijk, O.F.M., and J. Hazelden Walker, *The Origins of the Modern Roman Liturgy* (London, 1960), pp. 16–17.

[12] The Sarum Ordinal is edited in Frere, II. This edition, however, represents the Ordinal before its revision in the mid-fourteenth century. The best available edition of the divine office according to the Use of Sarum for reference in connection with Chaucer is the sixteenth-century printed edition of the Sarum Breviary edited by Procter and Wordsworth. In this edition, the rubrics are according to the revised Sarum Ordinal.

[13] Listed by John Beleth (fl. 1182), *Rationale divinorum officiorum*, in J.-P. Migne, *Patrologiae cursus completus*, Series Latina, CCII, Paris, 1855, cols. 13–166.

[14] See above, pp. 27, 36–7.

[15] For discussion, see van Dijk and Walker, pp. 26–44; 113–76; 213–37.

[16] Edmund Bishop, "On the Origin of the Prymer," in *The Prymer or Lay Folks' Prayer Book*, ed. Henry Littlehales, Early English Text Soc., O. S., No. 109 (London, 1897), p. xliii. The title is misleading: it is the translation, not the primer itself, which is for laymen. This version is according to the Use of Sarum.

[17] "Little Office of Our Lady," *The Catholic Encyclopedia*, IX, 294, col. 2.

[18] *The Hours of Jeanne D'Évreux Queen of France* (New York, 1957), p. 13.

[19] *Chaucer's Nuns*, p. 30.

[20] "Echoes of Childermas in the Tale of the Prioress," in *Chaucer: Modern Essays in Criticism*, ed. Edward Wagenknecht (New York, 1959), pp. 88–97; revised and reprinted from *MLR*, XXXIV (1939), 1–8.

[21] Willi Apel, *Gregorian Chant* (Bloomington, Ind., 1958), pp. 189–90.

[22] Legg, p. 32.

[23] *Loc. cit.* Legg gives only cues. This is common in the case of medieval missals, as lessons and gospels were read from special books. The translation here used is that of Lasance and Walsh, pp. 154–55.

[24] Legg, p. 32; Lasance and Walsh, pp. 155–56.

[25] Legg, p. 33; Lasance and Walsh, p. 157.

[26] See above, p. 35.

[27] See above, p. 48.

EPILOGUE

This study has followed the organizational pattern of the liturgy as Chaucer is likely to have known it under the Use of Sarum. The object has not been to hunt down every liturgical allusion in his works, though many are discussed in full, but to identify attitudes in his manner of speaking about the Church's ceremonies and the anniversaries of the ecclesiastical year which they commemorate. Some conclusions about Chaucer himself have already been drawn. It now remains to summarize these and to view them in retrospect.

To begin with, his dealings with the liturgy show very clearly what is widely recognized among scholars: that he was neither a zealot in Wyclif's cause nor an orthodox ascetic. While he disapproved of contemporary ritualism as did Wyclif, and while it is certain that he personally condemned clerical abuse of the sacraments for economic gain, these things do not of themselves constitute an attitude toward Catholicism as such. Far more important are the wit and predominant secularity of his treatment of the liturgy. These cannot be explained away by his own claim that he must be realistic. His oaths by saints' names are needed more often for rime than for realism, and they are clearly not the product of a mind that had religious devotion or reform as its first purpose. His references to holy days are more often than not to their secular merrymaking, while his references to the sacraments seldom describe ceremony except in social criticism and in fun.

The picture, nevertheless, is not that of an unbeliever, for the attitudes in question are common in societies predominantly Catholic. Many people believe in their religion and yet make light of it in jests which can be very crude. Chaucer's literary references to the liturgy show him to have been this kind of person: a sophisticated believer whose outlook on religion was secular. At the same time, he could write of the liturgy with reverence and with beauty as in the prologues of his two nuns. If indeed his basic attitude must be described as secular, he was, as a poet, greatly influenced by the language of the liturgy, which is itself a kind of poetry.

BIBLIOGRAPHY

Alexander of Villa Dei. *The Ecclesiale of Alexander of Villa Dei*, ed. and trans. L. R. Lind. Lawrence (Kans.), 1958.

Alighieri, Dante. *The Divine Comedy*, trans. Laurence Binyon, in *The Portable Dante*, ed. Paolo Milano. New York, 1947.

Apel, Willi. *Gregorian Chant*. Bloomington (Ind.), 1958.

Baum, Paull F. *Chaucer: A Critical Appreciation*. Durham (N. C.), 1958.

(Bede). *Venerabilis Baedae historia ecclesiastica gentis Anglorum*, in *Venerabilis Baedae opera historica*, ed. Charles Plummer. 2 vols. Oxford, 1896.

Beleth, John. *Rationale divinorum officiorum*, in *Patrologiae cursus completus*, Series Latina, ed. J.-P. Migne (222 vols., Paris, 1844–1905), CCII, 1855, cols. 13–166.

Binyon, Laurence. See Alighieri.

Bishop, Edmund. "On the Origin of the Prymer," in *The Prymer or Lay Folks' Prayer Book*, ed. Henry Littlehales. Early English Text Soc., O.S., No. 109 (London, 1897), pp. xi–xxxiii.

Boccaccio, Giovanni. *The Filostrato of Giovanni Boccaccio*, ed. and trans. Nathaniel Edward Griffin and Arthur Beckwith Myrick. Philadelphia, 1929.

Boyd, Beverly. "The Wife of Bath's Gay 'Lente'," *American Notes and Queries*, I (1963), 85–6.

———, ed. *The Middle English Miracles of the Virgin*. San Marino (Calif.), 1964.

Britt, Matthew, O.S.B., ed. *The Hymns of the Breviary and Missal.* 2nd ed. revised. New York, 1955.

Brown, Carleton. "The Prologue of Chaucer's 'Lyf of Seint Cecilie'," *MP*, IX (1911), 1–16.

The Catholic Encyclopedia. New York, 1910.

Caxton, William. See Jacobus de Voragine.

Chaucer, Geoffrey. Editions:
Donaldson, E. T. *Chaucer's Poetry: An Anthology for the Modern Reader.* New York, 1958.
Robinson, F. N. *The Works of Geoffrey Chaucer.* 2nd ed. Boston, 1957.
Skeat, Walter W. *The Complete Works of Geoffrey Chaucer.* 6 vols. Oxford, 1894.

Chilton, Eleanor Carroll, and Herbert Agar. *The Garment of Praise.* Garden City (N. Y.), 1929.

Coulton, G. G. *Chaucer and His England.* London, 1908.

Delehaye, Hippolyte. *The Legends of the Saints,* trans. Donald Attwater. New York, 1962.

De Worde, Wynkyn. *Nova legenda Anglie,* ed. Carl Horstman (*sic*). 2 vols. Oxford, 1901.

Donaldson, E. T. See Chaucer.

Duchesne, L. *Christian Worship,* trans. M. L. McClure. 5th ed. London, 1949.

Dugdale, William. *The History of St. Paul's Cathedral in London.* London, 1658.

Ellis, F. S. See Caxton.

The Encyclopaedia Britannica. 11th ed. Cambridge, 1910.

Explanatory Supplement to the Astronomical Ephemeris. . . . See Nautical Almanac Offices.

Fortescue, Adrian. "Liturgical Books," *The Catholic Encyclopedia*, IX, 296 (col. 2)–304 (col. 1).

———. "Liturgy," *CE*, IX, 306 (col. 1)–313 (col. 2).

Frere, W. H. *The Use of Sarum.* 2 vols. Cambridge, 1898, 1901.

Furnivall, F. J., Edmund Brock, and W. A. Clouston, eds. *Originals and Analogues of Some of Chaucer's Canterbury Tales.* Chaucer Soc., 2nd Ser., Nos. 7, 10, 15, 20, 22. London, 1872–87.

Gaylord, Alan T. "The Unconquered Tale of the Prioress," *Papers of the Michigan Academy of Science, Arts, and Letters*, XLVII (1962), 613–32.

Gerould, Gordon Hall. "Chaucer's Calendar of Saints," in *Chaucerian Essays.* Princeton, 1952, pp. 3–32.

———. *Saints' Legends.* Boston and New York, 1916.

Goddard, H. C. "Chaucer's Legend of Good Women," *JEGP*, VII (1908), 87–129; VIII (1909), 47–112.

Gower, John. *Confessio amantis,* ed. Reinhold Pauli. 3 vols. London, 1857.

Graesse, Theodor. See Jacobus de Voragine.

Griffin, Nathaniel Edward. See Boccaccio.

Guillaume de Deguilleville. *Le Pelerinage de Vie Humaine de Guillaume de Deguileville,* ed. J. J. Stürzinger. London, 1893.

Gunther, R. T. *Early Science in Oxford.* 11 vols. (Imprint varies), 1920–32.

Hamilton, Marie P. "Echoes of Childermas in the Tale of the Prioress," *MLR*, XXXIV (1939), 1–8; revised and reprinted in *Chaucer: Modern Essays in Criticism,* ed. Edward Wagenknecht, New York, 1959, pp. 88–97.

Hampson, R. T. *Medii Aevi kalendarium.* 2 vols. London, 1841.

Hill, J. W. F. *Medieval Lincoln*. Cambridge, 1948.

Hinckley, Henry Barrett. *Notes on Chaucer*. Northampton (Mass.), 1907.

Holweck, F. G. "Feasts," *The Catholic Encyclopedia*, VI, 21 (col. 2)–23 (col. 2).

Horstmann, Carl. See de Worde.

Huxley, Aldous. *Essays New and Old*. New York, 1927.

Ives, Doris V. "'A Man of Religion'," *MLR*, XXVII (1932), 144–48.

Jacobus de Voragine.
   Edition: Graesse, Theodor. *Jacobi a Voragine legenda aurea*. 2nd ed. Leipzig, 1850.
   Translations:
      Caxton, William. *The Golden Legend; or, Lives of the Saints as Englished by William Caxton*, ed. F. S. Ellis. 7 vols. London, 1900.
      Jehan de Vignay. *Legenda aurea sanctorum* (French). Paris, Antoine Vérard, 1493.
      Ryan, Granger, and Helmut Ripperger, *The Golden Legend*. 2 vols. London, 1941.

Jehan de Vignay. See Jacobus de Voragine.

Jenner, Henry. "Gallican Rite," *The Catholic Encyclopedia*, VI, 357 (col. 1)–365 (col. 2).

John of Tynemouth. See de Worde.

Jones, R. T. See *Sir Gawain and the Green Knight*.

Lasance, F. X., and Francis Augustine Walsh, O.S.B., eds. *The New Roman Missal*. New York, 1937.

Legg, John Wickham, ed. *Missale ad usum ecclesie Westmonasteriensis*. Henry Bradshaw Soc., Nos. 1, 5, 12. London, 1891, 1893, 1896.

———. *The Sarum Missal*. Oxford, 1916.

Lind, L. R. See Alexander of Villa Dei.

Littlehales, Henry, ed. *The Prymer or Lay Folks' Prayer Book.* Early English Text Soc., O. S., Nos. 105, 109. London, 1895, 1897.

Loomis, Roger S. "Was Chaucer a Laodicean?" *Essays and Studies in Honor of Carleton Brown.* New York, 1940, pp. 129–48.

Lounsbury, Thomas R. *Studies in Chaucer.* 3 vols. New York, 1892.

Lowes, John Livingston. "The Date of Chaucer's *Troilus and Criseyde*," *PMLA,* XXIII (1908), 285–306.

———. "The Second Nun's Prologue, Alanus, and Macrobius," *MP,* XV (1917–18), 1–10.

Madeleva, Sister M. "Chaucer's Nuns," in *Chaucer's Nuns and Other Essays.* New York, 1925, pp. 3–42; reprinted in *A Lost Language and Other Essays on Chaucer,* New York, 1951, pp. 31–60.

Maskell, William. *The Ancient Liturgy of the Church of England.* 3rd ed. Oxford, 1882.

———. *Monumenta ritualia ecclesiae Anglicanae.* 3 vols. London, 1846 (I, II), 1847 (III).

Matthew, F. D. See Wyclif.

Migne, J.-P. See Beleth.

Milano, Paolo. See Alighieri.

Moore, Arthur K. "'Somer' and 'Lenten' as Terms for Spring," *NQ,* CXCIV (1949), 82 (col. 1)–83 (col. 1).

Murata, Yuzaburo. "The Swearings in Chaucer," *Studies in English Grammar and Linguistics* (Otsuka Festschrift), Tokyo, 1958, pp. 289–99.

Murray, James A. H., ed. *A New English Dictionary on Historical Principles.* 10 vols. Oxford, 1888–1928.

Nautical Almanac Offices of the United Kingdom and the United States of America. *Explanatory Supplement to the Astronomical Ephemeris and the American Ephemeris and Nautical Almanac.* London, 1961.

O'Connor, J. J. "The Astronomical Dating of Chaucer's *Troilus,*" *JEGP,* LV (1956), 556–62.

Paden, W. D. "Jacques de Vitry, the Mensa Philosophica, Hödeken, and Tennyson," *Journal of American Folklore,* LVIII (1945), 44, n. 32.

Pauli, Reinhold. See Gower.

Plummer, Charles. See Bede.

Pollard, A. W., and G. R. Redgrave. *A Short-Title Catalogue of Books Printed in England, Scotland, & Ireland and of English Books Printed Abroad 1475–1640.* London, 1926.

Pratt, Robert A. "Chaucer Borrowing from Himself," *MLQ,* VII (1946), 259–64.

Procter, Francis, and Christopher Wordsworth, eds. *Breviarium ad usum insignis ecclesie Sarum.* 3 vols. Cambridge, 1882 (I), 1879 (II), 1886 (III).

Reilly, Cyril A. "Chaucer's Second Nun's Tale: Tiburce's Visit to Pope Urban," *MLN,* LXIX (1954), 37–9.

Robinson, F. N. See Chaucer.

Rock, Daniel. *The Church of Our Fathers.* 2nd ed. 4 vols. London, 1903 (I–III), 1904 (IV).

Root, Robert Kilburn. *The Poetry of Chaucer.* Boston, 1906.

———, and Henry Norris Russell. "A Planetary Date for Chaucer's *Troilus,*" *PMLA,* XXXIX (1924), 48–63.

Rorimer, James J., ed. *The Hours of Jeanne D'Évreux Queen of France.* New York, 1957.

Ryan, Granger. See Jacobus de Voragine.

"St. Erkenwald," ed. Henry L. Savage. *Yale Studies in English,* LXXII, New Haven, 1926.

(Sarum Breviary). See Procter.

(Sarum Legendary). *Legende totius anni tam de tempore quam de sanctis secundum ordinem Sarisburiensis.* Paris, 1518.

(Sarum Missal). See Legg.

Savage, Henry L. See "St. Erkenwald."

Schoeck, Richard J. "Chaucer's Prioress: Mercy and Tender Heart," in *Chaucer Criticism,* ed. Richard J. Schoeck and Jerome Taylor. 2 vols. Notre Dame (Ind.), 1960, I, 245–58.

Simpson, W. Sparrow. *Documents Illustrating the History of S. Paul's Cathedral.* Westminster, 1880.

Sir Gawain and the Green Knight. Editions:
Jones, R. T. *Sir Gawain and the Grene Gome.* Natal, 1960.
Tolkein, J. R. R., and E. V. Gordon. *Sir Gawain & the Green Knight.* Oxford, 1960.

Skeat, Walter W. See Chaucer.

Stürzinger, J. J. See Guillaume de Deguilleville.

Tatlock, John S. P. "Chaucer and the *Legenda Aurea,*" *MLN,* XLV (1930), 296–98.

———. "Chaucer and Wyclif," *MP,* XIV (1916–17), 65–76.

———. "The Date of the *Troilus:* and Minor Chauceriana," *MLN,* L (1935), 277–96.

———. "The Source of the Legend, and Other Chauceriana," *SP,* XVIII (1921), 419–28.

Thompson, Stith. *The Folktale*. New York, 1951.

Thoms, William J. *Early English Prose Romances*. New York, 1907.

Tolhurst, J. B. L., ed. *The Ordinale and Customary of the Benedictine Nuns of Barking Abbey*. Henry Bradshaw Soc., Nos. 65, 66, London, 1926, 1927.

Tolkein, J. R. R. See *Sir Gawain and the Green Knight*.

Van Dijk, S. J. P., O.F.M., and J. Hazelden Walker. *The Origins of the Modern Roman Liturgy*. London, 1960.

Wagenknecht, Edward. See Hamilton.

Wells, John Edwin. *A Manual of Writings in Middle English 1050–1400*. New Haven, 1916.

Wells, Minnie E. "The *South English Legendary* in Its Relation to the *Legenda Aurea*," *PMLA*, LI (1936), 337–40.

Wilson, P. W. *The Romance of the Calendar*. New York, 1937.

Wormald, Francis, ed. *English Benedictine Kalendars after A.D. 1100*. Henry Bradshaw Soc., Nos. 77, 81. London, 1939, 1946.

————. *English Kalendars before A.D. 1100*. HBS, No. 72. London, 1934.

Wyclif, John. *The English Works of Wyclif*, ed. F. D. Matthew. Early English Text Soc., O. S., No. 74. London, 1880.

INDEX

"ABC," 9, 10, 17
Absolon. *See* Miller, tale of
Alcestis, 36–7
Alexander of Villa Dei, 10
Alighieri, Dante, 29–30, 31, 32
Alison, the Carpenter's wife. *See* Miller, tale of
Alison, the Wife of Bath. *See* Wife of Bath
Alma Redemptoris Mater, 64, 65
Anne of Bohemia, 12, 14
Antiphoner. *See* Liturgical books
Antiphons (anthems), 61, 68
Anti-Semitism, 60
Augustine, St., Archbishop of Canterbury, 3

Bailly, Harry, 19, 38–9
Baptism, 47–9
Baum, Paull F., 60
Bede, 3
Benedict, St., Rule of, 63
Benedictines, 22
Bernard, St., 29–32 *passim*
Bible, 65
Boccaccio. 24n7
Book of the Duchess, 37–8
Braybrooke, Robert, 5–6
Breviary. *See* Liturgical books
Brown, Carleton, 29, 33

Caesar, Julius, 14
Calends, 10
Cambyses. *See* Summoner, tale of
Canonical hours, 2, 27, 60–73 *passim. See also* Liturgical books
Canterbury Tales. See individual entries
Capgrave, John, 43n22
Caxton, William, 34, 36
Cecilia, St. *See* Second Nun, tale of
Chauntecleer. *See* Nun's Priest, tale of
Chilton, Eleanor Carroll, 45
Christmas, 18–19
Clare, St., 38, 39, 40
Clergeon. *See* Prioress, tale of
Clerk: prologue of, 19; tale of, 55

Clifford, Richard, 5, 6
Confessio amantis, 37–8
Confirmation, 48–9
Confiteor, 49–50, 58n20
Constance. *See* Man of Law, tale of
Coulton, G. G., 45
Courtly love, 37–8, 49–50, 57
Cupid, 36–7, 49–50

Dan John. *See* Shipman, tale of
Dante. *See* Alighieri, Dante
Deguilleville, Guillaume de, 9, 17, 23n1
Derived rites. *See* Roman Rite
Devil, 35–6, 43n27
De Worde, Wynkyn, 43n22
Divine office, 27, 33, 64–8 *passim*
Dominical letters, 11–14
Donaldson, E. T., 60
Doxology, 68
Dugdale, William, 5
Dunstan, St., 35–6, 43n27

Easter, 3, 14–15, 20
Ecclesiale, 10
Edward, St., 34
Eglentyne, Madame. *See* Prioress
Erkenwald, St., 6, 23
Eucharist. *See* Mass
Ex ore infantium, 69–72

Fortunatus, Venantius, 32
Franklin, tale of, 18
Friar: portrait of, 50; tale of, 39, 54
Frydeswyde, St., 40

Gallican Rite, 2, 3
Gerould, Gordon Hall, 22, 27, 34, 40
Goddard, H. C., 36
God of Love. *See* Cupid
Golden numbers, 14–15
Gower, John, 37–8
Gregorian reforms. *See* Trent, Council of
Gregory the Great, Pope, 2–3
Griselda. *See* Clerk, tale of
Guilielmus Peraldus, 50

86

Hagiography, 26, 28, 36, 38, 60, 67
Hamilton, Marie P., 68–9
Hebdomadal letters, 11, 14
Hinckley, Henry Barrett, 47
Horae (primer). *See* Liturgical books
Host. *See* Bailly, Harry
Hours, book of (primer). *See* Liturgical books
Hours, canonical. *See* Canonical hours
House of Fame, 39
Hugh the Younger of Lincoln, St., 28, 35, 71, 72
Huxley, Aldous, 45

Ides, 10
Innocents, Holy, 61, 68–72
Introit. *See* Mass
Ives, Doris V., 46

Jacobus de Voragine, 29, 35
January, Chaucer's. *See* Merchant, tale of
Jehan de Vignay, 29
Joan, mother of Richard II, 21
John of Gaunt, 21
John of Tynemouth, 34
John the Baptist, 21, 35
Julian calendar, 9, 10, 14

Kenelm, St., 34

Legenda aurea, 29, 34, 35, 36, 42n9
Legendary (lectionary, martyrology). *See* Liturgical books
Legend of Good Women, 26, 36–8, 43n28, 50, 65
Lent, 15–16, 19–20, 25n16, 25n19
Little office of the Blessed Virgin Mary, 31–3, 64–9 *passim*
Liturgical books: calendars in, 9; character of, 1, 2, 3, 65, 66, 69; derived rites and, 3–4
  Volumes: antiphoner, 61, 64, 65, 68; breviary (*porthors*), 33, 65; legendary (lectionary, martyrology), 27, 36–7, 65; missal, 22–3, 68–71; ordinal (ordinale), 4–5, 47, 65, 74n12; primer

(*horae*, book of hours), 61, 66–8 *passim;* sacramentary, 3
Liturgical year. *See Temporale*
Lollards, 46–7
London, 5, 22–3
Loomis, Roger S., 45–6
Lounsbury, Thomas R., 45
Lowes, John Livingston, 12, 14
Loy (Eligius), St., 38, 39, 40
Lynne, Nicholas [of], 21
Lytlington, Nicholas, 22–3

Madeleva, Sister M., 60, 61–2, 67
"Madrian," 28, 38–40 *passim*
Man of Law, tale of, 19, 35, 36, 48
Martyrology. *See* Liturgical books
Mary, St., the Egyptian, 35
Mary, St., the Magdalene, 35
Mary, St., the Virgin, 9, 21–2, 28, 29–32 *passim*, 38, 60, 64–71 *passim*
Maskell, William, 4, 54
Mass: literary references to, 52–4, 62, 69–71; liturgy of, 2, 51, 53–4, 69–71; of derived rites, 3–4, 51, 68–71; of special occasions, 51–2, 56, 61, 68–72. *See also* Liturgical books
Matins, 62, 67–9
Matrimony, liturgy of, 20, 54–6
May, Chaucer's. *See* Merchant, tale of
Melibee, Tale of, 38
Merchant, tale of, 52, 55–6, 63
Metonic cycle, 14–15
Miller, tale of, 18, 40, 52, 53, 57, 64
Miracle plays, 20
Miracles of the Virgin. *See* Hagiography
Missal. *See* Liturgical books
Monk, prologue of, 28, 34–5, 38

Nicholas, St., 35, 71, 72
Nicholas the clerk. *See* Miller, tale of
Nones, 10
Nun's Priest, tale of, 18, 34

Oaths, 38–41, 46
O'Connor, J. J., 13
"Of Feigned Contemplative Life." *See* Wyclif, John

87